C000049490

In the Name of the Game

~

J.J. Barrett

First Published in 1997
by The Dub Press,
Amber, Violet Hill,
Herbert Road,
Bray,
Co. Wicklow,
Ireland.
Phone 01 276 1579
Fax 01 286 2708

Copyright (C) 1997, J J Barrett.

British Library Cataloguing in Publication Data.

IN THE NAME OF THE GAME

Barrett. J J

ISBN 0-9527-9236-2 hardback edition
ISBN 0-9527-9235-4 paperback edition

LEGAL NOTICE

J.J. Barrett

Son of the famous Joe Barrett of Kerry football fame (holder of six All Ireland medals), J.J. was born in Tralee in 1943 and he too played for Kerry in four All Ireland Finals, collecting one Senior and one U21 medal.

He is very much a Kerryman but as Dublin Gaelic Games correspondent of the Evening Herald he displays his love for football and hurling prominently on everything he writes about a subject very dear to his heart.

In 1996 J.J. Barrett published a successful book of poetry, *Not for Dedalus.*

As a result of a tender incident with his dying father in 1952, J.J. Barrett received the inspiration to write *In the Name of the Game*, a powerful mixture of turbulent history and Gaelic football which sheds new light on a critical time in Irish political and sporting history.

Acknowledgements

After playing a good match one sometimes got the odd few pats on the back. More often than not though it was an ample helping of appropriate abuse for missing a score, or committing some other cardinal sin of our games of football and hurling.

Now that the book is completed and before you, I must admit I have no abuse to dish out at all. However, I have many to thank for running in from the line with the magic bottle and resuscitating me as the game headed into injury time. There never was a more welcome final whistle.

My son, Joe Barrett, played a blinder for a whole summer holiday of his life. His discipline and editorial construction skills gave me a crucial lead midway through the second half.

Sean O'Mahony's encouragement, overall advice, and assistance was priceless as one floundered dangerously close to the inherent pitfalls of writing a first history book.

There were others too who kicked vital scores to lift the team as spirits flagged in the face of heavy odds and tough opposition.

I am forever indebted to the following team: My wife, Anne Barrett, who encouraged me to take on this task many years ago, and to Mícheál Walsh (Knocknagoshel), Sean and Bernadette Quilter (Florida), Tim Pat Coogan, Paddy Downey, Michael Kenny (National Museum of Ireland), Liam Mulcahy (Evening Herald, Dublin), John Joe 'Purty' Landers, Johnny Walsh, Tim O'Donnell, Gerry Brosnan and family (Moyvane), Bill Heffernan, Brian Sheehy, Niall Sheehy, Cormac Casey, Elsie Kerins O'Connor, Lena Kerins, Maurice Dowling, Paddy Conway, Bertie Conway, Tina Conway, Michael Costello (Kerry Co Library, Tralee), Danny Lynch (PRO, GAA, Croke Park), Padraig Kennelly (Kerry's Eye, Tralee), Paudi Fuller, The Kerryman Ltd., Dan Bally Keating, P J Cunningham, Denis Fitzgerald, Tomo Costelloe, Jack Waters, Jack Kirby, Miriam Malone and Angela Stephenson (daughters of the late Aloyisia Doyle (O'Brien)) and Paul Doyle (Tralee).

Despite its remarkable growth and development since the end of the nineteenth century, the Gaelic Athletic Association has been given scant attention by historians. This book serves to give an insight into the divisions and the atrocities of the Civil War period in Kerry and of the remarkable role played by the devotion to the club and county in bringing about peace and reconciliation. It is a fascinating read, penned with devotion and in a very readable format. While the Kerry experience may have been exceptional, similar stories could be told about players from other counties, who set aside their differences in pursuit of the All Ireland. The author has paid due credit to his father and his father's generation of brave Kerrymen. In the process, he has done a great service to the G.A.A.

Tá súil agam go mbeidh léitheoireacht fairsing ag an leabhar seo.

Liam Ó Maolmhicíl
Ard-Stiúrthóir
Cumann Lúthchleas Gael

Contents

Author's Note

I was first exposed to the seed of this book when as a nine year old in the spring of 1952 my father asked me to take a rolled black velvet cloth from the bottom of his wardrobe. It contained every honour in Gaelic football. He was forty nine. He was dying from a high blood pressure related complication, to which he succumbed just a few weeks later on June 2nd.

On that day the embryo was planted. From then on there grew a fanatical love for the game and an enthusiasm to follow in my father's footsteps on the field of play. The enthusiasm was easier than following in his footsteps.

Some years later I felt an ambition to write, to explain just what the games of Hurling and Gaelic Football mean to so many, and to illustrate what the games have withstood in pressure from without and within, to reach their present heady heights in popularity. The modern state-of-the-art Croke Park Stadium is testament to the enormous achievements of the GAA in its history, where it is now the last great amateur sporting organisation in the world. It is a long way from the days when my father and his team mates togged out in Barry's Hotel and walked in their football gear to play in Croke Park.

This contribution to its history is written enthusiastically in praise of the GAA and the people who make it. For the GAA has been, and is still, a whipping boy for every left wing, right wing, anti-nationalist, fascist, so called liberal and, of course, every expert at every pub corner or public house. Sometimes the criticism is valid but overall the contribution made by the GAA to Irish society and culture to date is unrivalled, and so often underrated, in the history of Ireland.

Current Irish Times sports writer, Tom Humphries captured the essence of the GAA in his book, Green Fields when he wrote:

"Nothing offers Ireland and the Irish such frequent cause for communal celebration as football and hurling, through every village, every parish, every town and every county the games are played and the sense of home is enhanced." [1]

This sense of home, village and county was handed on to me on that lovely day in 1952. It was the most impressionable and moving experience in my short relationship with my father. From that wrapped piece of velvet, on that warm spring day, my dying father held his football medals, which he wanted to see, for the last time.

The memory of a brave, dying man of forty nine, brought to tears as he examined and handled each medal, has stayed with me through all the years. He would finger one of his six All Ireland medals, look at the date, think a little and replace it. I have thought in my adult years that it was probably the first time Joe Barrett had ever handled or actually paid much attention to those same medals. This poem I penned recalls a most devastating event in the life of any young person, when he loses a parent. Coincidentally, it was a former great football colleague and friend, John Joe (Purty) Landers, one of the six profiled in this book, who came to break the bad news of Joe's death. I have attempted to recapture those traumatic days for me as a boy, and their later significance in the following lines:

"A Little Bag of Memories"

"The voice at the front door
Brought my mother some
Sad, bad news, at midnight.
Purty Landers had come
To tell the young woman
And her four children
That his old Kerry team mate,
Our father and my young mother's husband
Joe Barrett, had just died.
He was 49 years old.

There was a huge funeral,
A guard of honour of

Rock Street Club, Kerry teams,
Old IRA comrades,
Wreaths, tears, handshakes,
Much sympathy, some hypocrisy,
Six volleys with spent shells
falling by his grave.
Eulogies, Priests, Bishops, Nuns,
And the Last Post bugler.

I was nine years old,
Seemed to have to look up
At everything and everyone
That day,
Except the coffin.
I looked down at that.
The tricolour flag, the football jersey and boots,
And the spent shells.

I remember well
The hollow thud
Of shovelled earth
On a timber box,
With its own, spent shell.
I think of
My mother's white cold hands
Gripping my younger sister
And myself tightly, protectingly,
Close to her.

In its next issue
The Kerryman reported
"Joe Barrett is dead" and
The tributes poured in,
And on, to my
Dead father,
And his six All Ireland medals.

Time passed on
The children grew up,
I often thought of
June 2nd 1952,
The void was
Never filled,
And the young widow
Did her job well.

She bore her cross
With dignity, love and care for us,
With memories of
Her short marriage
To a famous man,
But six All Ireland medals
Don't put food on the table
Or buy an education.

Before he died
On a precious day
When he and I
Were alone together,
I sat on his bed
And we talked,
"I want you to
Take out a little
Bag from the bottom
Of the wardrobe, boy," my father said.
He took out each medal
And handled it.
He would look
At the date
On the back,
And silently he replayed
Many historic matches,
All Irelands, Leagues, County Championships,
Railway Cups and Tailteann Games.

To a child's mind
It meant little,
And medals meant nothing,
In fact,
I had never seen them before,
And now,
They seemed to make
My father weep.
This I did not like.

This year, 1987,
He is dead
Thirty five years.
His reputation and fame
Diminished by time,
His body by clay.

But the bond
Between a dying father
Of forty-nine
And his nine year old son,
Will survive the grave,
The years, and beyond,
Through an incident
With a little bag of memories,
From the bottom of the wardrobe,
Long ago in Kerry,
When I was young." [2]

From this traumatic but preciously tender experience with my father was born for me the first realisation of the importance and conscious significance of Gaelic games in my legacy. The games would dominate my life both positively and negatively for decades to come - the good times and bad, the wins and frustrating losses, the summer holidays forsaken, devoted to football. The constant of knowing that every Sunday of the year is tied up with the game. And training taking up too many week nights also.

On the road through Abbeyfeale about ten years ago garage owner, Neilus Mulcahy was selling me petrol when we realised we knew each other. Neilus passed a most profound remark which has stayed with me ever since. "Christ man, weren't you lucky too, that you stayed on playing long enough to have played with Sheehy, Power and Johnno." It was the truest word ever said to me, because those club years with the emerging young stars compensated for some miserable losses experienced on the inter county scene when Galway trounced Kerry in the mid-sixties.

Indeed, life in the game produced so many marvellous friendships carved out of sickening losses and exhilarating victories. The dressing room smells of sweat and embrocation. The craic with players like Billy Curtin, John Barry, Timmie Sheehan, Ger Power, Mikey Sheehy, Tommy "Bracker" O'Regan, Jackie Power Jnr., Fintan Lawlor, Teddy Brick, Paddy (Whacker) Moriarty, Tommy Kennington, Noel Kelter, young Colm Mangan, and twins Terry, and the late Rory McSweeny RIP, of Austin Stack's is memorable. The magic of being an 18 year old member of the Kerry dressing room, and in full-time training in 1962 with such greats as Mick O'Connell, Mick O'Dwyer, Tom Long, Paudie Sheehy RIP, Tim Tiger Lyons RIP, Seamus Murphy, Johnny Culloty, Kevin Coffey, Garry McMahon and Dan McAuliffe lives on. Marking such outstanding players as the towering John Dowling, Teddy O'Dowd, Denis O'Sullivan, Donie O'Sullivan, Gerald O'Sullivan and so many other names from Kerry's football story. The friendship and affection for the ever good humoured, roguish, but deadly competitive Niall Sheehy, carrying Sam Maguire to hostelries all over North Kerry with the late Timmie O'Sullivan. The friendship forged with the Lucey brothers, Jimmy RIP, Noel, Vincent and Paul of Glencar. Memories of good days when John O'Keeffe and Denis Long towered for us at midfield. Seeing the emergence of the young Ger O'Keeffe, Tony O'Keeffe and Mike and Paud McCarthy from Oakpark when we were relying on the great hearted Garry Scollard to lead young players down to 'Stack's from that area. All treasured memories.

Great times were spent on both sides of the Atlantic with the incomparable John Kerry O'Donnell. The abiding memories of the great Limerick hurler Jackie Power as our manager at Stack's. Of Dr. Eamonn O'Sullivan the originator of all modern team management.

At present I am enjoying the life of a full-time GAA journalist in Dublin where so many warm, strong friendships have been forged. I had played against many of the greats but never knew them socially at that time. It wasn't done to socialise with the opposition in those days in the sixties. Since then I have had many great times over a drink with my old sparring partner from the 1965 All Ireland Semi-Final, Lar Foley. And with my good friend Noel Curran of Meath and his son Paul of Dublin.

It had been a marvellous experience to play against such household names as Kevin Heffernan, Des Foley, Des Ferguson, John Timmons, Tony Hanahoe, Jimmy Keaveney, Mickey Whelan, Mick Kissane, Paddy Delaney, Paddy Holden, Billy Morgan, Jack and Martin Quinn, Sean O'Neill, James McCartan, Bosco McDermott, Enda Colleran, John Donnellan, John Keenan, Mattie McDonagh, and the great Noel Tierney. Getting to know many of these great GAA people has enriched my life.

Just as did a term as manager of Clara in Offaly when my colleague and close friend, P. J. Cunningham prevailed on me to take over the team as rivals Ferbane dominated Offaly football. In the shadow of the incredibly successful Ferbane management of Tony McTague and Kevin Gavin we built a team which went on to win leagues and championships after a famine of a quarter of a century. To the Reynolds brothers, Larry O'Carroll, Pat Flanagan, Barry Cowan, Padraig Moran, John Naughton, Mick Sheridan, but above all, P.J. Cunningham, I say thanks for the great memories. This was the legacy which Joe Barrett passed on to me from his sick bed when I was almost nine.

It is my contention that but for the GAA Ireland would have lost its identity in the twentieth century.

J.J. Barrett

PREFACE

The Wheatear is a migratory bird which flies back to Kerry from south of the Sahara Desert in March each year. The evolution of this bird innately tells it Kerry is a lovely, peaceful place in which to nest and produce its young. March 1923 was different. When the Ides dawned, many young men had died terrible deaths. By April Fool's Day there would be a toll of 28 Civil War killings for the month of March and the Wheatear hadn't even yet begun to build its nest.

The atrocities perpetrated in such placenames as Ballyseedy, Knocknagoshel, Countess Bridge and Bahaghs, Caherciveen would be indelibly marked on the subconscious of a whole generation of Kerry people.

It was thought the legacy which that month brought to Kerry would never be forgotten. But, now, after 74 years, the bitterness and hatred has been buried forever. Only monuments and faint memories remain after the cooling waters of the healing process eventually flowed cleansingly over a people. The Wheatear returns to a now peaceful Kerry and the people are united again.

This is a story of war, football, peace and reconciliation which affected Kerry footballers in some of the most terrible times this country has known.

It is the story of six exceptional men in the history of Irish sport and politics. In the shadow of the aftermath of the bloody War of Independence and the atrocity-filled Civil War, six men, amongst others, were a shining example of how Gaelic football was instrumental in the reconciliation of a divided Kerry.

Right through the turbulent twenties, thirties and even into the forties, these men put political differences aside for the sake of their beloved Gaelic football. Amongst them were the various shades of green and political hues, from a Free State Army Officer, to IRA men and a Garda.

In their lifetimes each became a household name. Many

other footballers contributed unsparingly to the healing but the extraordinary collective story of Con Brosnan, John Joe Sheehy, John Joe (Purty) Landers, Tim O'Donnell, Johnny Walsh and Joe Barrett had to be recorded lest their unstinting effort for county and country be forgotten for ever.

This book is dedicated to these men, and to all footballers and hurlers of that period who put politics aside to play their games, and to all people of reconciliation.

INTRODUCTION

This is a book about war and peace, but when writing his epic novel Leo Tolstoy could not have imagined the powerful role which sport would play as a third dimension in reconciling a bitterly divided people. The war was the Irish Civil War, the sport was Gaelic football and the people were the people of County Kerry.

In Tolstoy's time sport was not the great social opiate that it is today and so the 19th century Russian writer could not have foretold the extent to which sport would universally rise in importance for 20th century society, or how big a part sport would play in healing the sores left by war when peace dripped slowly on to a wounded Ireland of the 1920s and '30s.

In the context of world sport the story you are reading is surely unique in what was achieved through the contribution made by a handful of sportsmen towards the rehabilitation of a people in a war-torn land.

It is a story of reconciliation inspired by Gaelic football where a shattered people needed some reason and some extraordinary heroes to reunite them in a common purpose. The bonding was gradual but took place in the two decades after the Civil War in Ireland.

That Kerry has a unique story to tell is purely circumstantial. The savagery of the Civil War in Kerry, as in other Munster counties, necessitated extraordinary degrees of reconciliation. And it was the success enjoyed by Kerry in Gaelic football in the two decades following the Civil War that proved instrumental in creating the atmosphere for healing.

Kerry was the last bastion of Republicanism to fall to Free State Government forces. It was only after Michael Collins sent in three shiploads of Dublin troops to recapture the isolated county from the rebels that the towns in Kerry fell to Government forces. Collins was killed that same month of August, 1922, but it took his troops almost a year of the most vicious fighting, executions and atrocious reprisals on both sides to secure the remaining Kerry countryside from the rule of the IRA. The struggle for Kerry proved to be one of the most bitterly fought, producing some of the worst atrocities of the Civil War.

Throughout the Civil War period of 1922 and 1923, hundreds of Kerry men and women were interned. Ironically, this contributed to the eventual dominance by Kerry over the Gaelic football scene in the twenties. As a means of maintaining fitness and discipline, an intense programme of football training was introduced in the internment camps by the internees. As a result, when the camps opened some of the greatest names in Kerry football history were released to do duty, this time on the playing fields for their county. From here, against heavy odds, the long and emotional process of reconciliation began.

To the great majority of the Irish people the Gaelic Athletic Association (GAA) has represented the central core of our cultural tradition. Because of this central role in our society the GAA was to play a major part in the movement for independence and in the post Civil War healing.

The late Padraig Puirseal, a prominent Gaelic games writer, summed up the excellent contribution of the GAA to the people of Ireland in his opening paragraph. Nobody could improve on the phrasing.

"On All Saints Day, November 1st, 1884, a small group of men met in the billiard room of Miss Hayes's Commercial Hotel, Thurles. There they formally founded 'The Gaelic Association for the Preservation and cultivation of National Pastimes', ever since known as the Gaelic Athletic Association or, more familiarly, the G.A.A. It was to become the most popular and powerful athletics body in Ireland with an influence on the entire trend and pattern of Irish life. From its inception it consistently strove to mould the national outlook to its own ideals, to reawaken a legitimate pride of race and to further the resurgence of the national spirit." [3]

Should a permanent peace ever come about in the "Six Counties" Gaelic games could play an important role in the healing process between all Irish people from the two traditions. After all, the flag of the Republic of Ireland embodies that aspiration where Orange and Green meet in peace.

In the 1920s Gaelic games in Kerry were instrumental in the eventual breaking down of the seemingly impossible walls of hatred. Could it happen again in Northern Ireland were the GAA to become the catalyst of the healing process? Consider if people were to follow a common national sporting interest based on the loyalty to their native county. The inter-county structure is a fundamental strength of the GAA. It engenders a unique loyalty to one's native county on this island.

The traditionalists of the GAA might be asked to yield a certain amount of the Nationalistic rituals which have been an intrinsic part of the Association for the past one hundred years. But, that may be a small price to pay for welcoming into the organisation our brethren from the Unionist tradition who have for so long been isolated from their native games. They have lost out on something so very uniquely Irish. The GAA, in turn, has also been deprived by the exclusion of such an enormous percentage of their very distinctive fellow countrymen and women. However, a proper examination of such a role for Gaelic games in Northern Ireland would necessitate a book in itself, the issues being so sensitive and complex. It would warrant in-depth study and exploration by the Irish and British Governments, the GAA and the various loyalist and nationalist interests.

Chapter 1

Something precious

The period in which the stars of Brosnan, Sheehy, Walsh, Landers, O'Donnell and Barrett had risen and in which they had won so much football fame with Kerry was the most tempestuous era in the history of modern Ireland and, of course, of Gaelic games. The Civil War had divided families. Brother fought brother, towns, villages and parishes in Kerry were split, as they were in many other counties where that war raged.

Before the War of Independence the GAA had been steadily growing in popularity though in Kerry in the last half of the second decade, the political involvement of local patriot and county footballer Austin Stack hampered its development. It struggled during the worst of the war but held firm after Bloody Sunday (November 21st, 1920) and made a martyr out of Michael Hogan of Tipperary who was shot in Croke Park on that day.

But, the greatest test the GAA survived in its 113 year history was the overcoming of politics, both violent and non-violent, by very diverse and polarised views and beliefs. In Ireland in those decades most people held strong political feelings one way or the other. The Nationalists had prevailed to see a twenty six county Free State Government rule after the Anglo-Irish War (The War of Independence) 1919 to 1921. The Anglo-Irish Treaty was signed in December 1921 and was to plunge the country into a civil war between the Pro and Anti Treaty supporters. People who had fought side by side and sacrificed greatly to defeat British rule were now divided and became deadly enemies. The Pro Treaty supporters followed Michael Collins, Arthur Griffith and William T. Cosgrave, while the Anti Treaty camp included such household names as Eamon de Valera, Liam Lynch, Rory O'Connor, Liam Mellows, Cathal Brugha, Erskine Childers, Sean Moylan, Tom Barry, Harry

Boland and Frank Aiken. Many of these outstanding Irish freedom fighters would perish at the hands of former comrades, as
did the great Collins himself.

The terrible animosity which this war created severely tested the multi-factioned nationalist membership of the GAA. But
the great majority controlled their more extreme political ten-
dencies, in the name of the game.

After the Civil War, in late 1923 and early '24 a group of
young Kerry men were released from the internment camps at
Hare Park and Tintown in the Curragh Camp. My father was
one of those released. A number of them won an All Ireland
Senior football medal within slightly over a year, after losing
the postponed 1923 All Ireland Final to Dublin in the meantime.

On that Kerry team were IRA members, Free State Army soldiers and other players who sympathised with the ruling
Cosgrave Government but would not have been actively
involved in politics.

After captaining Kerry to All Ireland victory in 1929 Joe
Barrett handed over his next captaincy in 1931 to Captain Con
Brosnan, a Free State Army Officer, who was a member of the
Army which had incarcerated Barrett in various locations for
almost a year and a half. Brosnan and Barrett played on opposing sides in the famous Ex-Internees versus Kerry match in
1924, which was to set the foundation stone for Kerry's successes of the 20s and even further ahead. This historic match
will be covered later in the book.

In his history of the GAA, de Burca described how the GAA
helped to heal the deep felt wounds inflicted on the people of
Ireland by the Civil War:

"When, in due course, the executions and the fighting ended
and the jail gates and the internment camps were opened, it
was under the neutral auspices of the Association that many an
old friendship which had been sundered by the Civil War
began once more to be rebuilt. Predictably, the Civil War, which

made such a lasting impact on the political and social life as a whole, also left some scars on the GAA. That it did not split the Association is little short of a miracle and a tribute to the loyalty of both officers and rank-and-file members." [4]

The friendship between Barrett and Brosnan, at one point political enemies, was to exemplify the healing powers of Gaelic football in Kerry. It was at its most visible when Barrett handed the Kerry captaincy to Brosnan in 1931. There was uproar in many quarters in Kerry, even in Barrett's own club, Rock Street (now Austin Stack's). But he remained determined, weathered that storm, was on the All Ireland team with Brosnan and was himself back as skipper again in 1932 when Kerry completed the four in a row.

The following turbulent years saw a loose rule of the gun, strikes, the threat of the growth of fascism under O'Duffy, who was a prominent GAA official from County Monaghan, and the Economic War with Britain. There followed a time when players were on the run, and Irish society was divided on issues of killings by the IRA. From then into the '40s, the people of Ireland would witness the execution of Republican prisoners and men on the run by the State. The firing squad, and even a hanging by the State, summary execution by both sides would ensue.

From 1920 to 1945 the 26 Counties went through incredible trauma as a society, but yet at Croke Park on Sundays there were growing attendance figures with very mixed political views. Notwithstanding this, they were drawn to the common bond of our National Games. During that time the "Ban" against British Army and RUC being members of the GAA was steadfastly enforced.

There was considerable pressure on county teams to stand down in sympathy with political causes. In 1924 Kerry refused to play the delayed 1923 All Ireland Final because the Chairman of the County Board was still in prison. The Cork County Board similarly supported their imprisoned chairman, Sean McCarthy. This action drew the support of Limerick and the other Munster counties and was soon followed by the support of the Connacht counties. The Central Council reacted with suspensions for dissenting counties and awarded walkovers to the teams they should have met. However, in July, when the remaining prisoners, including Eamon de Valera, Austin Stack, and Sean McCarthy, were released the impasse was broken and the suspensions were lifted. On September 28, 1924, Kerry lost that 1923 All Ireland football Final to Dublin by 1-5 to 1-3. [5]

It was a difficult time for the Gardai and the Irish Army who were resented in some areas in the games, but all through, a hard core of "belief" in Gaelic games was to successfully keep the political issues apart. Damage to the game was largely avoided, while the healing of Civil War wounds progressed through the common love for the game.

This book will attempt to deal with many delicate issues. I will use some case studies and, in fact, put forward the suggestion that contrary to much unhealthy critical opinion of the GAA, Gaelic games are, and have always been, while loyal to the national beliefs, open and unbigoted.

I have interviewed a number of the surviving great names from the era in question, including the last few remaining political prisoner/ footballers who experienced and now recall what it meant to play football for Kerry during the turbulent era from the 1920s to the 1940s.

Chapter Notes (pages 4 - 21)

(1) Humphries, Tom, Green Fields, writer's note.

(2) Barrett, J J, Not For Dedalus, p7.

(3) Puirseal, The GAA In Its Time, p10.

(4) De Burca, Marcus, The GAA A History, p163.

(5) Ibid p 164, 165. also in Munster GAA Story, by Jim Cronin p125 and 126.

Chapter 2

Climate

The Kerry of today is a much different place from the Kerry of the late 19th century, the Kerry in which the generation who witnessed and took part in both the War of Independence and the Civil War were reared. One could argue that generally and for most of the population the standard of living has risen dramatically. Not having lived through or even near these times it must be very difficult for the teenager or young adult of today to visualise the hardship seen by most Irish people raised in Ireland in the early and mid part of this century.

In an effort to aid those unfamiliar with the times, in this chapter, I will try to recreate some of the chief aspects of the culture into which that generation of the late 19th century was born. Though this book is primarily about the reconciliation of a divided Kerry generation, the author will endeavour to outline some of the principal events which their parents and grand parents lived through, or even witnessed at first hand. In a way it is an effort to unwrap and expose, if possible, some of the primary influences on the outlook of the people, hence the culture into which the characters in this book were nurtured.

The reader may say there were obvious landmark events even prior to this time which would certainly have coloured the consciousness of the people further. However, an expansion of this theme would, to my mind, fall outside the scope of this book. The period I am interested in is the years that would have been witnessed by both the War of Independence generation and their immediate ancestors on the grounds that the social climate would be more influenced by current events witnessed first hand. I acknowledge, however, that I am possibly taking some liberty here. I am happy to let the historian decide.

To understand some of the obstacles they overcame in their achievements one must appreciate that communications between town and country were limited to horse, bicycle and steam railway service. Up to the mid-19th century the post was often carried on foot. Local folklore maintains that post from Tralee to Castleisland was carried by a local blind man who knew the road well, an eleven mile journey.[1]

There was also the unique mono-railed Lartigue railway line running between Listowel and Ballybunion. The main railway system had been extended to Tralee in 1859 and certainly was an improvement on the horse drawn coach which took half the day to travel to Killarney. By the turn of the century there was a rail service linking the main towns of the county, Tralee, Killarney, Cahirciveen, Dingle, Listowel, Kenmare, Castleisland, Castlegregory and Fenit Port. However, by this time there were very few motor cars and only a handful of telephones had found their way into use.

The Royal Irish Constabulary (RIC) Barracks kept the law in most villages and towns, while the largest British Military Garrison was situated at Ballymullen Barracks in the town of Tralee, to enforce the laws of the Crown.

Generally, much poverty was evident in the towns, while in rural Kerry the smallholder community worked hard to eke a frugal existence.[2] By 1841, Kerry had a population of over 400 to the square mile of arable land. Kerry was essentially an agricultural community. Due to the practice of sub-division, small holdings were a feature of this agrarian society. Employment and means of survival from the land ranged from being the owner of the big house, to peasant farmers, to labourer on the land or if lucky, having a secure job at the "big house".[3]

Hard currency was scarce and only the very well-off could afford to pay their staff in cash. The small farmer paid his labourers in kind, by allowing them a strip of land on which to grow their own potatoes. This fact proved detrimental during the famine as, ironically, the towns such as Tralee enjoyed much prosperity in trade and had ample stock of food but those who needed it most did not have the necessary cash for which to buy it.[4]

There was a limited number of substantial farmers in the north of the county and at the top of the social scale, the Big House landlord class, the professional class, the merchants and their servants formed an almost self-sustaining sector of their own ilk. This minority of Kerry people enjoyed a good standard of living and comforts, most unrepresentative of the majority of the people in the county. This trend continued into the 20th century.

Having reviewed the extensive historical research done on Kerry focusing on the 19th and early 20th century, it is evident that the plight of the poor was largely unchanged during this period. They tended to be the first to suffer in times of disaster, from a particularly bad winter to the devastation of the Great Famine. One such example was the year 1847, a year that was particularly cold, with snow and storms adding to the famine troubles of the population. The destitute from the countryside had to walk into Tralee, then containing the only two workhouses in Kerry. Some travelled more than thirty miles and those who reached their destination arrived in a diseased, starved and wretched state. [5]

It is interesting to note, according to research, that the poor of the time believed the Great Famine to be the will of God and would not have been overly aware that their plight was partly due to the economic philosophy of the government of the time,[6] who were not too concerned with the fate of the Irish peasant, and partly due to a dependent and impoverished situation with few resources to cope with such a plight.

While some great effort was made by sections of the wealthy in Kerry, it appears that the powers-that-be saw famine along the lines of such popular economists as Thomas Malthus and Nassau Senior, to whom a famine was merely a natural population check. They believed that Ireland suffered from overpopulation. Ireland's poverty was seen as a threat to Britain's prosperity. [7]

Therefore, despite the hardship endured by people in Kerry during the Famine, violence and uprising were not common occurrences. Generally, apathy and fatalism appeared to have clouded the Kerry person's spirit.[8] However, in Blennerville, Gateway to Tralee's Past, the authors of the book give an account of the proceedings of one example of unrest.

"On the 6th of November, 1847, an attack on the workhouse was launched. A few people from the labouring class left Strand Street, in Tralee, led by a man holding a black flag. As they passed through the streets they were joined by others, and on reaching the workhouse they numbered about two hundred. They were becoming more and more aggressive and eventually burst in the front door of the workhouse. A small force of police which had arrived had no effect whatsoever. On calming down the masses...the crowd demanded "outdoor relief". This action was the result of the demoralising effect of the temporary relief system."[9]

It would appear that any intervention by Britain in the early or mid 19th century poverty in Ireland was motivated not from concern or pity for the wretched Irish but from an ulterior motive. According to John Douglas who wrote a paper in 1828, entitled, "Observations on the necessity of legal provision for the Irish Poor": he expressed a "desire to protect all classes in Britain from the degrading competition of Irish pauper labour, and the consequent augmentation of the pressures of pauperism on British soil and capital."[10]

And while these victims may have pointed to Divine Providence, succeeding generations would become more suspicious of any claims that Britain was genuinely concerned or willing to help the Irish.

On a large and widespread scale, lack of food, heat and appropriate clothing was a general health hazard for the deprived in both 19th and early 20th century Ireland. A recorded case in point was a newspaper account in The Kerry Evening Post, detailing the effects of the harsh winter of 1901 on the poor of Kerry. It gives one some idea of the extent of the poverty prevalent in the Kerry of that time.

"Rarely has the winter told with so much severity on the

poor as this present year. The biting inclemency of the season and the great and continued dearth of employment have reduced the humbler classes to a sad condition indeed. In the cities and larger towns many noble and combined efforts are being made to afford timely relief. It is no exaggeration to say, however, that in the rural districts the poorer farmers and labourers are quite as much at the mercy of the elements, and in many instances quite as destitute as the poor who live in the lanes of our cities." [11]

The Great Famine

Kerry was hit hard by the Great Famine and Tralee being the county's chief town was inevitably going to be faced with crisis situation. It was forced to play host to the thousands of refugees who flocked into the town.

As mentioned earlier the poor suffered most, or to be put more sociologically, the counties with the lowest incomes per capita, and the highest rate of illiteracy, had the greatest excess mortality. The annual rates of excess mortality, per thousand, by county, for the period 1846-1851 showed Kerry to be third hardest hit of the counties only after Mayo at 58.4 and Fermanagh at 29.2. Kerry showed a rate of 22.4. [12]. And according to MacLysaght, who, it is acknowledged, produced a thoroughly researched series of papers on the Great Famine, Castleisland and the Desmond Barony was notably one of the worst afflicted in the county.

In an effort to sustain themselves people turned to eating shellfish, various seaweeds, nettles, dandelions and fern roots. MacLysaght also claimed that the Kerry people even ate frogs in their struggle to survive. Ironically, this is now a 20th century delicacy with the culinary knowledge of preparation. [13]

There were two principal workhouses in Kerry at the height of the Great Famine. One at Ballyard, a mile on the Dingle side of Tralee, and the other at Rathass, a mile outside the eastern side of Tralee. These represented the nearest source of State

assistance. Should the workhouse at Ballyard be full, the fam-
ished and fever-ridden people would struggle on to the
Rathass workhouse. The track was known locally as Cosan na
Marbh - The Track of Death. Such pitiful sights lingered in the
minds of locals for generations to come. Death stalked every
lane and alley in Tralee. [14]

It is acknowledged that the massive tide of migration to
Tralee, from these and other surrounding areas, in anticipation
of relief and employment, during and after the famine, drained
the town of its previous prosperity.

One mile west of Tralee lies what was then Blennerville Port,
and from here many thousands emigrated on Famine ships to
avoid the catastrophic conditions prevailing in Kerry at the
time. Local merchant, Nicholas Donovan, commissioned a ship
in Quebec City in 1847 at the height of the coffin ship period.
Named, The Jeanie Johnson, the 100 foot long converted cargo
ship accommodated up to 220 passengers in steerage and con-
centrated mainly on emigrant runs to Canada, where a 100 acre
farm could be purchased for £8-15s (£8.75 in today's money).
The Tralee ship would then return with a cargo of timber.
Throughout her career as an emigrant vessel she never lost a
passenger while at sea. [15] My grandfather, Tim Barrett, who
was born in 1881 had an old song about the emigrant days of
the Jeanie Johnson. Unfortunately, only these few lines of the
song remain:

"And how was I to know,
that my loved one was to go,
on the Jeanie from Tralee.

It is generally acknowledged that Kerry suffered badly from
the potato blight. One primary source and witness to this dis-
astrous time in Irish history, which the author was fortunate
enough to have come across, is a diary and a first hand account
of the famine by one Robert O'Kelly. Born on the June 18th,
1835, in the town of Castleisland, and reared in Tralee, Mr

O'Kelly, whose father was born in 1798, gives us some graphic feelings of the period.

Robert O'Kelly is the grandfather of Aloyisia Doyle, nee O'Brien, of Tralee who was an old family friend of my mother, Kitty. She received this hand written journal belonging to Robert O'Kelly from Mrs Doyle who also came from a very old Tralee family, as can be seen from her grandfather's journal.

"THE GREAT FAMINE OF '46 AND '47

IT IS WELL I REMEMBER THOSE YEARS OF MISERY AND STARVATION. THE PEOPLE DYING OF HUNGER ON THE PUBLIC STREET AND IN THE PUBLIC ROADS EVERY DAY. WHERE IT WAS DEATH FROM HUNGER AND STARVATION, THE GREAT MAJORITY OF THE PEOPLE IN THOSE DAYS WERE POOR AND THEY HAD NO FOOD OF ANY KIND TO SUSTAIN LIFE IN THEM ONLY PULLING THE WILD WEEDS AND NETTLES AND BOILING THEM MIXED WITH A GRAIN OF AGE-BLOWN MEAL TO SUSTAIN LIFE IN THEM. FAMILIES LEFT THEIR HOMES AND LAND AND WENT TO THE TOWNS BEGGING FOR FOOD TO KEEP LIFE IN THEMSELVES AND THEIR FAMILY AND TRIED HARD TO PROVIDE FOOD TO KEEP LIFE IN THEM. ONLY ONE INSTANCE I KNEW.

A FARMER, HIS NAME WAS PATRICK O'BRIEN, FINE TYPE OF MAN, SIX FEET HIGH, LEAVE HIS FARM, HE HAD GRASS FOR TWELVE COWS. HE HAD SEVEN DAUGHTERS AND HIS WIFE, A FINE FAMILY. EVERYTHING ON THE FARM WAS SOLD TO BUY FOOD TO KEEP THE FAMILY ALIVE. HE WAS OBLIGED TO LEAVE HOME AND LAND BEHIND AND COME INTO THE TOWN BEGGING FOR SOMETHING TO EAT FOR HIS STARVING FAMILY. I COULD NEVER FORGET THE SIGHT I SEE IN THIS FAMILY AND HUNDREDS OF OTHER FAMILIES. THEY WERE ALL EMACIATED WITH THE HUNGER, THE BONES OF THEIR BODIES PROJECTING THROUGH. I HAVE SEEN THAT FAMILY AND HUNDREDS OF OTHERS EATING THE BOILED NETTLES TO KEEP LIFE IN THEM FOR IT WAS MY FATHER AND MOTHER'S HOUSE THEY GOT SHELTER FROM THE INCLEMENCY OF THE NIGHT, WHERE THEY RESTED FOR A WEEK OF NIGHTS AFTER THE HARDSHIPS OF THE DAY TRYING HARD TO PROVIDE SOMETHING TO EAT FOR HIS CHILDREN. THE FOLLOWING WEEK HE LEFT HIMSELF, AND SEVEN DAUGHTERS DIED ON THE SIDE OF THE PUBLIC ROAD IN ONE DAY TOGETHER, AND BURIED WITHOUT COFFINS IN ONE GRAVE. THE MOTHER SURVIVED BUT GOT OFF HER HEAD. THERE WAS NO

MAN SEE MORE OF THE HUNGER, MISERY AND STARVATION IN FAMILIES THAN I DID IN THOSE YEARS. IT WAS THE SAME ALL OVER THE COUNTRY IN EVERY PLACE, IN TOWN, VILLAGE AND THE COUNTRY AROUND.

EVERYWHERE YOU TURNED IN THOSE YEARS YOU MET DEATH, DEATH FROM SHEER STARVATION AND HUNGER. THERE WAS NOTHING TALKED OF THOSE DAYS BUT DEATH. HERE, THERE AND EVERY PLACE, MEN AND WOMEN IN THE FULL PRIME OF LIFE GOING DOWN TO THEIR GRAVES FROM HUNGER AND STARVATION. NO WHERE OR PLACE TO GET A MORSEL OF FOOD TO KEEP THE LIFE IN THEM. IT WAS A PITIABLE SIGHT FOR ANY HUMAN BEING TO LOOK AT AND SEE THE SIGHTS THAT I HAVE SEEN IN THE POOR AND POVERTY STRICK- EN OF GOD'S CREATURES IN THOSE YEARS. IT WAS SOMETHING TERRIBLE AND AWFUL TO BEHOLD AND LOOK AT DEATH, DEATH EVERYWHERE AND IN EVERY PLACE, WITHOUT COFFINS GOING DOWN TO THEIR GRAVES. IN THOSE DAYS THE POOR COULD NOT PROVIDE COFFINS SO THAT THOUSANDS CONSIGNED TO THEIR GRAVES WITHOUT COFFINS. I GRIEVE TO SAY THAT I HAVE SEEN ALL THIS IN MY DAY WITH MY EYES OPEN TO ALL THE SIGHTS, SCENES THAT IN THOSE SAD AND SORROWFUL YEARS TOO NUMEROUS TO MENTION OR RECALL, ALL SCENES THAT IN THOSE YEARS OCCURRED FOR THEY WERE MOST REVOLTING TO HUMANITY NO MATTER HOW HARDENED THE PERSON WAS THAT WIT- NESSED THEM.

I FERVENTLY HOPE AND PRAY TO THE GOOD, MERCIFUL AND THE GREAT GOD THAT HE MAY NEVER AGAIN VISIT HIS OWN PEOPLE IN SUCH A DIRE FORM AS HE DID IN THOSE YEARS AND NEVER AGAIN DURING THE LIFETIME OF THIS WORLD TO COME, IF IT BE THE WILL OF THE MOST HIGH.

I MUST WRITE IN TRUTH AND RECORD IT HERE AS WITNESS, THAT MY FATHER AND MOTHER DURING THOSE YEARS '46 AND '47 NEVER REFUSED A NIGHT'S SHELTER TO ANY ONE WHO CAME THE WAY LOOKING FOR IT. THERE'S SCARCELY A NIGHT DURING THOSE YEARS THAT SOME ONE FAMILY, 2, 3, 4, 5 OR 6 FAMILIES CAME DURING THOSE YEARS. THEY HAD TWO OUT-HOUSES WITH A FIRE PLACE IN EACH HOUSE. THEY KEPT A SPLENDID TURF FIRE IN EACH TO WARM THOSE POOR STARVING OF GOD'S CREATURES AFTER THE HARDSHIPS OF THE DAY WITH PLENTY OF CLEAN STRAW TO MAKE A KIND OF A BED FOR THEM. ANYONE OR FAMILY THAT COULD NOT PROCURE A NIGHT'S SHELTER WAS DIRECTED TO GO DOWN TO MORTIMER O'KELLY. WHAT THEY DONE AT NIGHT FOR THOSE STARVING CREATURES I KNOW NOT BUT I KNOW THEIR CHARITY WAS UNBOUNDED IN THOSE SAD YEARS OF MISERY, HUNGER

AND STARVATION. WHAT THEY HAD THEY GAVE WITH A FREE HAND AND GOOD HEART FOR GOD.

OH WHAT SCENES I WITNESSED AT NIGHT CARRYING THE TURF TO KEEP THE FIRE FOR THEM. IN EACH OF THOSE HOUSES SOME HAD SOMETHING AFTER THE DAY TO PUT ON THE FIRE AND OTHERS HAD NOTHING WHEREWITH TO SOIL THEIR LIPS. THOSE SCENES ARE AS PLAIN TO ME TODAY AS WHEN I WENT AMONGST THEM. THEY COULD NEVER BE FORGOTTEN BY ANY PERSON WHO WITNESSED THEM. I WAS A GOOD STRONG BOY AT THAT TIME. I WAS TWO YEARS AT COOPERING TRADE SO MY RECOLLECTION OF THOSE YEARS CANNOT BE QUESTIONED FOR I HAVE PASSED THROUGH THEM BEING THEN 11-12 YEARS."

Robert O'Kelly went into great detail about his involvement in the town of Tralee and even traced his great grandfather's time in the town where he was born at Moyderwell Cross in the seventeenth century. When he completed this diary, the last two paragraphs he finished thus:

"THERE WAS NO ONE IN TRALEE AND ITS SURROUNDINGS WEAK MINDED ENOUGH TO BECOME INFORMER, ALTHOUGH THE ORGANISATION (THE FENIANS) COMPRISED HUNDREDS OF GOOD MEN AND TRUE FROM 1863 TO 1867.

THANK GOD I HAVE LIVED TO SEE THE HOME RULE BILL ON THE STATUTE BOOKS, THE LAW OF THE LAND FOR FUTURE GENERATIONS TO COME ON THIS DAY 15TH SEPTEMBER, 1914. GOD SAVE IRELAND." [16]

Home Rule was not to come in Robert O'Kelly's lifetime. He obviously had realised that it is better to be in charge of one's own country and affairs, especially when capitalism by its very nature defines self-interest as normal. Thus being ruled by a foreign capitalist power, with the landlord system of the time was abhorrent to people such as Robert O'Kelly. The devastation of the famine, the memories of the penal system and the injustices of landlordism underlined this fact of life for him.

While illiteracy was high in Ireland in the mid 19th century, the ancient medium of word-of-mouth, and indeed first-hand experience by people like Robert O'Kelly must have built up a deep distrust of having Irish internal affairs handled by an outside power.

One of our leading scholars, Prof. J.J. Lee, claims that some of the intentions of the education system of the mid nineteenth century, as outlined below, did not succeed. It is interesting to note what those intentions aimed to introduce:

"A MASSIVE BRAINWASHING OPERATION, OBLITERATING SUBVERSIVE ANCESTRAL INFLUENCE BY INCULCATING IN THE PUPILS, A PROPER REVERENCE FOR THE ENGLISH CONNECTION, AND A PROPER DEFERENCE FOR THEIR SOCIAL SUPERIORS, DEFINED ACCORDING TO THE ENGLISH CONCEPT OF CLASS". [17]

However, it seems, if Robert O'Kelly was any way typical of a man's consciousness of that time, education was sought after as a means of escape from hard manual labour.

"I AM THE SEVENTH IN THE GENERATION IN THE COOPERING TRADE IN MY FAMILY. THE MONEY EARNED OUT OF IT WAS BY HARD SWEAT AND GREAT LABOUR. THE SHIRT ON YOUR BACK NEVER DRIED DURING THE DAY OR WEEK.

SCHOOLING NOW-A-DAYS IS IN EVERY CORNER OF THE COUNTRY AROUND, THANK GOD. WHEN IN MY YOUNG DAYS, 75 YEARS AGO THERE WAS NO SCHOOLS ONLY PROTESTANT SCHOOLS. THE ONLY SCHOOLS FOR CATHOLIC CHILDREN WERE THE HEDGE SCHOOLS AND IT WAS NOT IN EVERY PLACE ONE OF THOSE SCHOOLS COULD BE FOUND. THEY WERE VERY RARE AND FAR APART. IT WAS AT ONE OF THESE SCHOOLS I MADE MY FIRST APPEARANCE UNDER A MAN NAMED JOHN DEVINE UNTIL THE NATIONAL SCHOOLS MADE THEIR APPEARANCE IN 1842. ALL THE YOUTH LIKE ME WERE FORCED TO GO TO THE HEDGE SCHOOLS, THERE WAS NO ALTERNATIVE OR STOP FROM GOING THERE.

IN 1842 THE NATIONAL SCHOOLS STARTED, IT WAS A GREAT BOON TO THE CHILDREN THEN LIVING. THERE WAS A GREAT MASTER GOT. THE FIRST APPOINTMENT A MAN, TIMOTHY HORAN. I WAS HIS REAL AND ONLY PET AT SCHOOL WHILE I WAS LEFT THERE. WHAT A CRIME IT WAS TO TAKE ME FROM IT." [18]

Landlordism

It is reasonable to say that an innate resentment to the landed gentry was present in most Kerry people, or even most Irish people in the decades leading up to the War of Independence. Memories of evictions, unreasonable taxes and run down estates due to absenteeism fuelled such resentment and distrust. As can be seen below, there were many well publicised cases exposing the exploitative aspects of the system of land-lordism in Kerry. They are included to illustrate the issues and feelings that would have been topics of conversation of the people of the times, hence contributing to the climate of that era into which leaders like Austin Stack and John Joe Sheehy were born.

In 1886, Land League founder, Michael Davitt told a gather-ing in Castleisland that in the previous three years, 1,600 fami-lies had been evicted in Kerry. [19]

Some accounts of the darker side of landlord policy in Kerry will be relayed. And while some decent landlords did exist, the following cases illustrate how the law was on the side of the land owner, thereby leaving the tenant totally at his mercy. Rents could be set at the discretion of the landlord and, as can be seen, the tenant had little effective recourse should the rent be too high.

The author selected Mr Trant Foley as a sample of the extent of the powers a landlord possessed, even into the 20th century. It shows how destructive he could be to the lives of his tenants if he so chose. He was also a good example of the animosity held towards things Irish and exemplified by some of those extremely loyal to the Crown at the time. A struggle between these classes was to ensue until history ran its course.

A typical example of this struggle is evident from the fol-lowing extract, published in the local newspaper, Kerry People, on the 10th of August, 1907:

"EVICTION NEAR TRALEE
SOME PERSONS FOOLISHLY IMAGINED THAT THE WORK OF EVICTION IS A THING OF THE PAST IN THIS COUNTRY; BUT SUCH, UNFORTUNATELY, IS NOT THE CASE. ON SATURDAY LAST MR. JEREMIAH O'SHEA, OF CLAHANE, WHOSE LANDLORD IS MR. PETER TRANT FOLEY, WAS EVICTED FROM HIS HOME. MR. O'SHEA, A VERY INDUSTRIOUS MAN, HAS GIVEN THE FOLLOWING PARTICULARS OF THE CASE TO OUR REPRESENTATIVE:-
I ENTERED THE LAND COURT TO HAVE A FAIR RENT FIXED BEFORE THE

SUB-COMMISSION, AND THE CASE WAS HEARD AFTER FOUR YEARS. THE SUB-COMMISSIONERS FIXED THE RENT AT £39 6S. YEARLY, AND PUT ON £8 3S. 9D. FOR PROXIMITY TO TRALEE, FOR 20 IRISH ACRES, THOUGH IN THE CASE OF ANOTHER FARMER WHO LIVES NEARER TRALEE THEY ONLY PUT ON £5 16S. FOR PROXIMITY, AND THE FARM CONTAINS 70 IRISH ACRES, GOOD LAND WITH SUBSTANTIAL BUILDINGS. I APPEALED TO THE DECISION OF THE SUB-COMMISSION, AND THE CASE WAS FINALLY HEARD (AFTER SEVEN YEARS) AT KILLARNEY, WHERE THE LANDLORD, MR. TRANT FOLEY, WHO WAS, AND IS, WELL AWARE THAT THE LAND IS NOT WORTH THE RENT, VALUED THE FARM AT £37, OR £1 AN ENGLISH ACRE. I ALSO DREW THE ATTENTION OF THE COMMISSION TO THE WRONG DONE TO ME ABOUT PROXIMITY TO TRALEE, BUT THEY TOOK NO NOTICE, AND FIXED THE RENT AT THE SAME FIGURE, THE VAL-UER FOR THE HEAD COMMISSION BEING MR. BOYD, DUBLIN. I COULD NO LONGER PAY THAT RENT, AND HAD TO SELL OFF A FEW COWS. I HAD TO PAY OTHER DEBTS. ABOUT THIS TIME A RECEIVER WAS APPOINTED OVER THE ESTATE, AND WROTE DEMANDING PAYMENT. I COULD NOT PAY, AND I WAS SERVED WITH A WRIT (KING'S BENCH). I OFFERED TO PAY A FAIR RENT, AND WROTE TO THE RECEIVER, BUT GOT NO REPLY UNTIL LAST SATURDAY, AUGUST 3RD, WHEN HE REPLIED BY SENDING A FORCE OF POLICE AND BAILIFFS, COM-MANDED BY MR. TRANT FOLEY, TO EVICT ME. I WAS ABSENT AT THE TIME, AND WHEN I RETURNED I FOUND MY WIFE AND FAMILY THROWN OUT, AND EVERY ARTICLE OF FURNITURE I POSSESSED, IN THE YARD. THERE WAS NO ONE PUT IN POSSESSION AS CARETAKER. I AM ENCAMPED A FEW YARDS AWAY, AND I MEAN TO STICK THERE UNTIL I GET THE LAND FOR A FAIR PRICE. I AM AT PRE-SENT EMPLOYED BY THE COUNTY COUNCIL." [20]

The following case is important to relay in that it shows the predicament a family was in should an eviction notice be issued. There was no court of human rights in that era in which to put one's case. The story is also important in that the press followed it as it developed, showing editorial policy to have its finger on the pulse of nationalist feelings in Kerry at the time.

It is perhaps one of the worst events to have occurred as part of the agrarian unrest, during the period 1904 - 1912. A classic example of man's inhumanity to man. It is also an important case in that this tragic act of exploitation of poor people made its way to the House of Commons.

The following article appeared in the Kerry Evening Post, in September, 1912:

"GLENBEIGH AGAIN!
HOUSE BURNING NEAR TRALEE
LANDLORDISM AT ITS WORST

ON TUESDAY LAST CAPTAIN TRANT FOLEY, AND BAILIFFS HOARE AND MCCARTHY, PROTECTED BY FIFTEEN POLICE, VISITED THE HOUSE OF DANIEL HANAFIN, WHICH IS SITUATED IN A VALLEY A SHORT DISTANCE FROM THE TOP OF THE HISTORIC MOUNTAIN OF GLEANN SCOHEEN - AND PROCEEDED TO EVICT HANAFIN, HIS AGED MOTHER AND SISTER.

THE SHERIFF WAS LOATH TO REMOVE THE OLD WOMAN, WHO WAS CONFINED TO BED, BUT THE GALLANT CAPTAIN INSISTED ON HER REMOVAL AND HASTENED TO GIVE EFFECT TO THE LAW, AND SAID HE WOULD TAKE THE RESPONSIBILITY ON HIMSELF. THEY THEN PROCEEDED TO REMOVE THE OLD WOMAN IN A SIDE-CAR TO THE HOUSE OF HER DAUGHTER, MRS. FOLEY, A DISTANCE OF ABOUT ONE MILE. IT WAS A SAD PROCESSION, AS THE OLD WOMAN, WHO IS OVER 80, WAS IN AN EXHAUSTED CONDITION. HOWEVER, THE GALLANT CAPTAIN CARRIED OUT THE MANOEUVRES SUCCESSFULLY.

THE RENT OF THE HOLDING IS £7 10s. AND LAND IS COMPRISED OF AN ACRE OR TWO, THE REMAINDER BEING A WILD MOUNTAIN.

HANAFIN OFFERED TO PAY £5 AS A FAIR RENT, BUT THE CAPTAIN DECLINED TO ACCEPT HIS OFFER.

AFTER REMOVING THE OLD WOMAN THEY CAME BACK, AND REMOVED THE FEW ARTICLES OF FURNITURE.

BUT THE EVICTION WAS NOT YET COMPLETE, AS CAPTAIN FOLEY PRODUCED A BOTTLE CONTAINING PARAFFIN OIL FROM HIS POCKET, POURED IT ON THE THATCH, AND SET IT ON FIRE.

THE SISTER TO THE TENANT PROTESTED AGAINST SETTING THE HOUSE ON FIRE, AND THE REPLY GIVEN BY FOLEY IN A STERN TONE WAS: "I CAN DO WHAT I LIKE WITH MY OWN." HE THEN ORDERED A BAILIFF TO THROW DOWN A PART OF THE WALL, AND WHEN THAT WAS DONE, THE EVICTION WAS COMPLETED, AND THE CAPTAIN MARCHED

AWAY WITH THE HONOURS OF WAR". [21]

Some weeks later, an article in the same paper titled *The Result of the Clahane Eviction* read:

"WE REGRET TO REPORT THE DEATH ON THE SEPTEMBER 27TH, OF THE OLD WOMAN, MRS. MARY HANAFIN, WHO WAS EVICTED FROM A SMALL FARM AT CLAHANE ON TUESDAY, 19TH SEPTEMBER.

THE PARTICULARS OF THE EVICTION ARE FRESH IN THE MINDS OF THE PUBLIC, AND REMIND US FORCIBLY OF THE SCENES IN GLENBEIGH, DURING THE EVICTIONS CARRIED OUT THERE IN THE EIGHTIES.

THE HOUSE WHERE THIS POOR OLD WOMAN LIVED WAS SET ON FIRE, SHE HAD BEEN REMOVED FROM THE BURNING BUILDING IN A FAINTING CONDITION, PLACED ON A SIDE-CAR, AND BOUND WITH A ROPE TO PREVENT HER FROM FALLING OFF - THE ROAD IN THIS PLACE BEING VERY ROUGH AND HILLY.

THOUGH EVERY ATTENTION WAS GIVEN TO THE OLD WOMAN SINCE HER REMOVAL, SHE NEVER RALLIED, AND DIED ON THE WEDNESDAY, 27TH ULT.

THE INTERMENT TOOK PLACE IN KILTALLAGH ON FRIDAY, AND WAS LARGELY ATTENDED BY FRIENDS AND NEIGHBOURS OF THE DECEASED." [22]

This case and the high degree of press coverage it received was to heighten the nationalist feelings in Kerry. The same landlord would get much satirical coverage as a result of this editorial interpretation of his deeds as can be seen below. Even poetry was used to the same effect.

Indeed, stories of successful resistance to landlord pressure would also have circulated, though not all too frequently did they happen. One such incident involved the Blasket Islanders against Lord Cork in 1906.

Although it had been a high point in the era of the bailiff and evictions, some boost for nationalist morale must have come in November of 1906 with the failed attempt by police and bailiffs to seize boats and other chattels of the Blasket Islanders, in satisfaction for arrears of rent said to be due to Lord Cork.

The following is an account of the event, published on the 13th of November, 1906:

"ISLANDERS TOO MANY FOR POLICE AND BAILIFFS

BLASQUET TENANT'S VICTORY

THE ELEMENTS, COUPLED WITH THEIR OWN DETERMINATION, HAVE WON ANOTHER AGRARIAN VICTORY FOR THE HARDY RESIDENTS OF THE BLEAK BLASQUET ISLANDS, OFF THE DINGLE PENINSULA.

FOR THE PAST FEW WEEKS, STATES OUR TRALEE CORRESPONDENT, QUITE A LITTLE ARMY OF POLICE AND BAILIFFS HAVE BEEN ENDEAVOURING TO MAKE A DESCENT ON THE ISLANDS, THEIR OBJECT BEING THE SEIZURE OF THE BOATS OR OTHER CHATTELS OF THE ISLANDERS IN SATISFACTION FOR ARREARS OF RENT SAID TO BE DUE TO LORD CORK AND HIS LATE FATHER FOR A PERIOD OF FOURTEEN YEARS. THE RENT CHARGED IS SAID TO BE AT THE RATE OF 40S A COW, WHILE THE TENANTS ARE REPORTED AS WILLING TO PAY AT THE RATE OF 8S PER COW; BUT THIS OFFER WAS NOT ACCEPTED.

OUR CORRESPONDENT RECALLS THAT OVER FORTY YEARS AGO A FORCE OF POLICE AND BAILIFFS MADE AN ABORTIVE ATTEMPT TO SEIZE FOR RENT, AND ABOUT EIGHTEEN YEARS AGO THE BAILIFFS ACCOMPANIED A FORCE TO THE ISLAND WITH A SIMILAR OBJECTIVE, BUT WITH NO GREATER SUCCESS.

THE LATEST ATTEMPT HAS ALSO PROVED A FAILURE. AFTER WEEKS OF WATCHING AND WAITING, THE POLICE FORCE HAVE RETURNED TO TRALEE WITHOUT HAVING MADE ANY SEIZURE. THE ISLANDERS, IT APPEARS, HAVE AS THEIR LEADER A MAN NAMED FLINT, AND HE, IT IS SAID, SIGNALLED TO THE MAINLAND A FEW DAYS AGO STATING HIS WILLINGNESS TO CONFER WITH THE REPRESENTATIVE OF THE CONGESTED DISTRICTS BOARD, WHO, IT IS UNDER-STOOD, OFFERED TO BUY OUT THE ISLAND AT NINETEEN AND A HALF YEARS' PURCHASE. THESE TERMS FOUND FAVOUR WITH THE TENANTS, AND, THANKS TO THE INTERVENTION OF THE KINDLY PARISH PRIEST OF BALLYFERRITER, THE REV. T. GRIFFIN, THERE IS NO LIKELIHOOD OF ANOTHER ATTEMPTED INVASION OF THE BLASQUETS (BLASKETS)." [23]

Such incidents must have contributed to fanning the flames of resentment, but also hope, amongst the "working classes" as the ordinary people saw their neighbours terribly wronged by the authorities and the wealthy while having no right of come-back through the recognised legal framework.

Some local newspapers did not spare the law enforcers and landlord class of the county as is evidenced by strong accounts of their high handed deeds.

While Irish Nationalists were beginning to unite and realise their strengths a little more, Capt. Trant Foley, nevertheless, continued his tactics against his tenants. In this next case, however, the tenants in question are of a rather curious nature, which, as shall be seen, added fuel to the fire of his critics:

"THE CAPTAIN AND THE GANDER

ON SUNDAY MORNING LAST CAPTAIN TRANT FOLEY, CARETAKER OF THE CLAHANE EVICTED FARM, LATELY IN THE OCCUPATION OF JEREMIAH O'SHEA, ACCOMPANIED BY BAILIFF HOARE, MADE AN IMPORTANT SEIZURE ON THE LANDS.

IT APPEARS THAT A GANDER, IN COMPANY WITH SIX OF HIS HAREM, WAS ACCUSTOMED TO FREQUENT THE VACANT FARM. SOMETIMES THEY WENT FOR NOURISHMENT, AT OTHER TIMES FOR RECREATION; IN A GENERAL WAY THEY WENT FOR A FLIRTATION, BUT AT ALL EVENTS, THEIR PRACTICE WAS INVARIABLY AGAINST THE LAW.

THE FEATHERED INTRUDERS HAD ALWAYS SUCCEEDED IN EVADING CAPTURE, BY REASON OF THE FACT THAT THEY HAD RECOURSE TO AVIATION WHEN THE GALLANT CAPTAIN MADE HIS APPEARANCE.

HOWEVER, THE "PLUCKING SEASON" ARRIVED, AND THE OWNER OF THE ADVENTUROUS BIPEDS IN A CRUEL, AND, AS IT HAPPENED, UNFORESEEN MANNER DEPRIVED THEM OF THEIR PINIONS, WITH THE RESULT THAT ON SUNDAY MORNING THEY HAD TO CAPITULATE HELPLESSLY AND HOPELESSLY.

THEY HISSED BRAVELY TO THE LAST, AND IT WAS ONLY WHEN THE SULTAN OF THE DEVOTED FLOCK WAS SEVERELY WOUNDED IN THE HEAD, AND RENDERED HORS DE COMBAT, THAT THEY SURRENDERED AT DISCRETION, AND WERE MARCHED WITH DROOPING AND SPIRITLESS WINGS TO THE SHERIFF'S POUND.

WE CONGRATULATE CAPTAIN TRANT FOLEY ON HIS ACHIEVEMENT. AS A FEATHER-BED WARRIOR AND ONE WHO HAS MASTERED THE INTRICATE GOOSE-STEP, IT IS APPROPRIATE THAT HIS FIRST REAL CAMPAIGN SHOULD BE AGAINST THE TRIBE WHICH HAS BEEN RESPONSIBLE FOR CASTING ODIUM AND RIDICULE ON THAT BRANCH OF THE MILITARY SERVICE WHICH HE ADORNS.

IN THE EVENT OF A GERMAN INVASION THERE IS NO DOUBT THAT A GRATEFUL BRITISH WAR OFFICE, COGNISANT OF CAPTAIN FOLEY'S ASININE

TACTICAL ACHIEVEMENT, WILL REMEMBER HIM WITH PRIDE AND ASSIGN HIM
TO A POSITION OF EMINENCE BE-FITTING THE CONQUEROR OF THE CLA-
HANE GANDER. "[24]

Arising out of the above incident came this rather amusing
poem:

THE GANDER OF CLAHANE

Oh, I was once a happy bird, and free from grief or care,
My name and fame were widely known with respect everywhere
O'er Clahane's fords and streams and woods, I wandered many a day
And none dare stop me in my flight and none dare say me nay.
I've lorded o'er the feathered tribe for many a good long year
Defending well my female kind and never knowing fear;
From Mangerton to Dingle Bay, from Fenit to Ahane
No prouder bird did soar the land than
THE GANDER OF CLAHANE.

But, alas, my trust in mankind proved the cause of my downfall,
For treacherous hands on me were laid, my feathers plucked and all;
My wings were clipped, my neck was cropped, well may I curse the fate
That left me helpless there where once I stood so proud and great.
My wives and all my relatives were treated just the same
The heads that once could rear so proud are drooping now with shame.
A poor, bedraggled, wretched bird, and not worth a Smihaan,
Is all that's left of me, the once proud
GANDER OF CLAHANE.

To hide my shame I gathered all my wretched, ruined clan
And refuge took on No Man's Land, to hide from face of man;
No man we knew did own the spot, no trespassers were we
Nor ever thought we'd be disturbed or e'er have cause to flee.
For a short time all was peacefulness, our hopes and aims an high,
We knew the time would not be long when we could once more fly,

And once again from Dingle Bay, from Fenit to Ahane
Would proudly ring the fierce war cry, of
THE GANDER OF CLAHANE.

But, alas! "The best laid plans of men and mice gang aft agly,"
A warrior bold named FOLEY came well armed from Tralee,
We found ourselves surrounded, though whenever shrank with fear

When called on to surrender by this gallant Fusilier.
We shouted back defiance, and we "badhy'm" do their worst,
We never would surrender to that bailiff band accursed.
But a wail is heard in Dingle, aye in Fenit and Ahane,
For a prisoner held by Foley is
THE GANDER OF CLAHANE. [25]

Despite such animosity being directed at Foley at every opportunity, it did not deter him from his campaign of harassment. One point, however, worthy of note at this stage, is that the small tenants and ordinary citizens of Kerry seemed to be getting bolder and more willing to take a stand against their oppressors. Evidence of this can be seen in the following article, published in the Kerry Evening Post, during the summer of 1912.

The following article shows Trant Foley's hostility to things Irish to the point of pettiness, a characteristic humorously pointed out by one reader below.

"MR. TRANT FOLEY'S ENGLISH

THE ATTEMPT OF MR. PETER TRANT FOLEY, J.P., AT THE LAST PETTY SESSIONS IN TRALEE TO DECRY THE IRISH LANGUAGE BY REFUSING TO RECEIVE A PLEDGE SIGNED IN IRISH BY THE REV. CHARLES BRENNAN, C.C., ON BEHALF OF A DEFENDANT, WILL SCARCELY COMMEND ITSELF TO IRISH IRELANDERS, THOUGH IT MAY FIND FAVOUR WITH THE KERRY MILITIA, OF WHICH HE IS A DISTINGUISHED WARRIOR. "WE SPEAK ENGLISH IN THIS COURT," HE SAID, "AND WE CANNOT TAKE ANYTHING THAT'S SIGNED IN IRISH." OF COURSE, MR. TRANT FOLEY'S KNOWLEDGE OF THE ENGLISH LANGUAGE IS VERY PRO-

FOUND. HIS KNOWLEDGE OF LAW IS EQUALLY ERUDITE; BUT WE WOULD SUG-
GEST THAT CRUDE IMPERTINENCE ON THE BENCH IS SCARCELY THE THING. IT
SHOULD BE STATED THAT MR. MICHAEL MCMAHON, J.P., M.C.C. DIS-
AGREED WITH MR. FOLEY IN HIS RULING." [26]

The following are the letters which came in response to the
above article, again giving, it is reasonable to suggest, an indi-
cation of what the editor believed representative of his reader-
ship:

"TRALEE MAGISTRATES AND THE IRISH LANGUAGE
TO THE EDITOR
ST. JOHN'S, 19:10:'07.
DEAR SIR, - I NOTICE THAT A SECTION OF THE TRALEE MAGISTRATES HAVE
RECENTLY REFUSED TO RECOGNISE A WRITTEN PLEDGE BECAUSE THE SIGNA-
TURE WAS IN IRISH. THIS REMINDS ME OF A BAILIFF WHO CONSIDERED THAT
IRISH WAS NOT "GENTEEL" ENOUGH FOR HIS CHILDREN. THE BAILIFFS ARE
LOSING THEIR OCCUPATION RECENTLY. CAN IT BE THAT THEY ARE BEING PRO-
MOTED TO THE BENCH?
MISE AGAT,
CATHAOIR UA BRAONAIN.

QUERY:- IF ONE WORD OF IRISH IS SUFFICIENT TO FRIGHTEN A MILITIAMAN,
HOW MANY REAL SOLDIERS WOULD RUN AWAY FROM FR. DINEEN'S
DICTIONARY?" [27]

As to whom the credit for this second letter should go, I'm
afraid I do not know, as the letter is not signed. It is, however,
in my opinion, worth printing nevertheless:

"WHO IS MR. P.T. FOLEY, J.P., OF TRALEE? AT THE TRALEE PETTY
SESSIONS THERE WERE TWO CHARGES OF DRUNKENNESS AGAINST SOME MAN
WHO PRODUCED A PLEDGE BEARING AN IRISH SIGNATURE. THIS MR. P.T.
FOLEY, AS REPORTED IN THE LOCAL PRESS, SAID: "WE SPEAK ENGLISH IN THIS
COURT, AND WE CANNOT TAKE ANYTHING THAT'S SIGNED IN IRISH." WHAT
HO! MR. P. ENGLISH FOLEY. PROBABLY THERE IS A GOOD DEAL OF INDIFFER-
ENT AND BROKEN ENGLISH SPOKEN ON THE BENCH OF THE TRALEE PETTY
SESSIONS, BUT EVEN IF THE JAY PEES WERE ALL ADDISONS, SO FAR AS THEIR

English was concerned, it does not at all follow that they should reject a document signed in Irish. That is merely ignorance, and Mr. P. English Foley, J.P., of Tralee, writes, or speaks, himself down a very ignorant man. If a document written and signed in French, where the nun hunters come from, were presented, we suppose P. English Foley, J.P., would spend half the night over a French-English dictionary in a wild endeavour to appear as one capable of reading "Frinch" on the "Binch" of Tralee, where the J.P.s "spake" English. Let us not be taken as having any sympathy for the drunkard who displayed a pledge signed in Irish. But the ignorance and boorishness of P. English Foley, J.P., of Tralee, ought to be subjected to a fine as well as drunkenness. We wonder what does the P. stand for? Surely it couldn't be for common Patrick, the name of a certain mere saint! It must be Percy or some novelette cognomen of that kind." [28]

Following the publication of the above, a statement was issued by the County Council of Kerry, which went as follows:

"IRISH LANGUAGE ACTION OF THE TRALEE MAGISTRATES

The following motion standing in the name of Mr. McD. Mahony was read:- "That we, the County Council of Kerry, take this opportunity - which is the first we have had since the occurrence - to emphatically protest against the action of the magistrates who sat at the Tralee Towns' improvement Court on Monday, October 14th, in refusing to accept a pledge because it was signed in Irish. That we are gratified to learn that Mr. McMahon, J.P., dissented from the action of the West British hirelings who sought to insult our national language, and that as we have always done what lay in our power to forward the language movement, so we, as the premier public body in the county, take this occasion to mark our indignation at such an occurrence." [29]

While it appears from the above that Trant Foley's hostility did not escape the notice of the press, he nevertheless maintained his position as aggressor, when it came to dealing with his tenants.

"EVICTION AT CAMP

On Saturday last Head Constable McGoldrick, in charge of a party of twenty police, afforded protection to Capt. Trant Foley, J.P., an employee in the Sub-Sheriff's office, and two bailiffs, when taking possession of four small plots of land at Camp. The plots are owned by four tenants who are not satisfied with the amount of compensation allowed in connection with alterations that are being carried out on the line. The decree for forcible possession was at the suit of the Committee of Management of the Tralee and Dingle Railway Company. Possession was peacefully handed over, only nine or ten little children witnessing the fierce array of police who escorted Captain Foley." [30]

And so the people seemed more than willing to doubt even further the goodwill of their rulers. The pot for revolution was on the boil and people like Austin Stack and Thomas Ashe, (Ashe later died on hunger strike), were being recognised as possible leaders for change.

Barrington's "Discovering Kerry", underlined the general lawlessness of Kerry in the late 19th century. [31] This showed the rampant discontent growing amongst the majority of the people in Kerry. The land war was raging and though landlordism was gradually to decline the evictions were leaving a sad trail of destruction.

A nationalist undercurrent was beginning to manifest itself in the first decade of the 20th century and the past urgings of Thomas Davis, Charles Stewart Parnell, the Land League, the Gaelic League and the Gaelic Athletic Association (GAA) had left their mark on those who were not too unconcerned to hear.

Although the Famine and its aftermath left Kerry decimated of a strong healthy male population in the mid 19th century, agrarian unrest and agitation began to gather momentum in the county. There had been a limited Fenian Rising in Kerry in

1867. The Moonlighters had been founded in Castleisland as a vigilante movement to oppose the curse of landlordism, but all of this activity had shown little effect on the ruling class.

As the hopes and dreams of a better way of life faded with the downfall and passing of Charles Stewart Parnell, and with the landlord class represented by people like the infamous Peter Trant Foley in Tralee, it is easy to see how and why Austin Stack found a willing, hungry land of discontent in which to sow the seed of revolution, and revulsion for the ruling classes.

Padraig Pearse addressed a large crowd in Tralee in June 1914 and again in February 1916, priming an upsurge of Republicanism which blossomed through the local branch of the Irish Volunteers. It was led by Austin Stack and ultimately spawned the strong beliefs which culminated in the horror of the terrible and tragic events of the Civil War in Kerry during March and April of black 1923.

Former Editor of The Kerryman newspaper, Con Casey, who was a veteran of both the War of Independence and the Civil War, and who escaped the sentence of death, told the author:

"The innate seed of defiance in Kerry may have been nurtured by a few Fenians and those who resisted in some way the heavy hand of the landlord but this glimmer of resistance was fertilised into a bright flame by Austin Stack. He was the one who got Kerry to stand up and be counted." [32]

While in sport, the GAA was beginning to express the culture of the Irish masses, though the fledgling GAA had yet to make its mark and though the north Kerry village of Ballyduff had won the All Ireland hurling championship of 1891, athletics, cycling and greyhound coursing were more popular among the farming and working classes. There was also a strong tradition of "garrison games" but access was restricted to the more well off. Rugby, hockey, cricket, tennis and fox hunting were the preserve of the upper classes.

This was the social climate of a Kerry in which football stars of the future Con Brosnan, John Joe Sheehy, Johnny Walsh, Joe Barrett, John Joe (Purty) Landers, Tim O'Donnell and their generation of Kerry footballers were to grow and mature in the first two decades of the century.

They came from divers backgrounds, and all would eventually take up very different political routes in life, but in the meantime they would come together to bring Kerry football its most important era in the illustrious history of the game in the Kingdom.

They were to live through the public revulsion of the executions of the 1916 Rising leaders. Many claim this awakened a feeling of national determination. Commandant General Tom Barry, the IRA hero of the War of Independence, was one such nationalist, although Kerry IRA leader, Tom McEllistrim, pointed to the introduction of the Bill to establish compulsory military service in Ireland in 1918 as his reason for firing the first shots of the War of Independence. [33]

Of our six main characters in this book, the older three, Con Brosnan, John Joe Sheehy and Joe Barrett fought in the War of Independence. Together with the three younger men, all six Kerry players would prove the power of sport in the horrific climate of civil war. It was to happen in the aftermath of a Civil War which tore the fabric of Kerry society to pieces and left open wounds between previously close friends and relatives. It might never have been healed if not for one common purpose, the success of Kerry in the game of Gaelic football. It would eventually act as a veritable bond for almost all Kerry people wherever they met throughout the world. The Civil War would be forgotten in the context of football.

I have endeavoured to extrapolate some of the more important events and circumstances in Kerry's history starting in the mid 19th century. My intention as outlined in the opening pages of this chapter was to paint a picture of the 19th century Irish experience. The realisation of which would lead to a cultural outlook conducive to a concerted effort for independence.

The years from 1916 to 1923 were to be the most turbulent in modern Irish history. Society, sport and politics would change drastically. Unity of family, village, parish, town and county would be tested to the extreme. These would be bleak years for Kerry football, in which no All Ireland medal came to the Kingdom.

Chapter Notes

(1) O'Dwyer, Michael. Tralee. A Historical Guide. p20.

(2) MacLysaght, W. The Great Famine in Kerry. 18/10/1958. In a series of articles in The Kerryman, October-November 1958.

(3) Ibid. 18/10/'58.

(4) Ibid. 1/11/'58.

(5) Ibid.

(6) Donnelly, James Jnr. A New History of Ireland. Vol V. Ireland Under The Union 1801 - 1870. Ed. W.E. Vaughan. New York, (1989). p356.

(7) Kinealy, Christine. The Role of the Irish Poor Law during the Famine. In Cathal Porteir. The Great Famine. Dublin. (1995). p104.

(8) Barrett, Mary. St Raphael's Magdalen Asylum, Tralee. A Case Study. Unpublished Thesis. UCG. (1996). p30.

(9) Kelly, Lucid and O'Sullivan. Blennerville, Gateway to Tralee's Past. (1989)

(10) Douglas, John. Observations on the necessity of a legal provision for the Irish Poor. Published by Wakeham, Dublin. (1828), p4.

(11) Kerry Evening Post, December 1907. In Peter Trant Foley's papers.

(12) Cousens, S.H. Regional death rates in Ireland during the Great Famine, from 1846 to 1851 in Population Studies, xiv, No. 1, July 1960. pp55-74.

(13) MacLysaght, W. The Kerryman. 25/10/'58.

(14) Barrett, Mary. p67.

(15) Laxton, Edward. The Famine Ships. 1996. p153.

(16) O'Kelly, Robert. Personal journal written in 1914.

(17) Lee, Joe. The Modernisation Of Irish Society 1848 To 1918. Dublin 1973. p28.

(18) O'Kelly, Robert.

(19) Barrington, T J. Discovering Kerry. (1976). p120.

(20) Kerry People. August 10th, 1907.

(21) Kerry Evening Post. September 1907.

(22) Kerry Evening Post. October 1907.

(23) Kerry Evening Post. November 1906.

(24) Unidentified local newspaper extracted from Trant Foley's diary, Tralee 1912.

(25) Ibid.

(26) Kerry Evening Post 1912.

(27) Kerry Evening Post October 1907.

(28) Ibid.

(29) Ibid.

(30) Kerry Evening Post. November 1907.

(31) Barrington, T J. Discovering Kerry. (1976) p120.

(32) Casey, Con. Former Editor The Kerryman newspaper.

(33) Dwyer, Ryle. The Kerryman article on late Tom McEllistrim, former Fianna Fail T.D., and War of Independence, Civil War veteran. (August 19, 1994).

Chapter 3

The Bleak Years 1914-1925

Kerry only began to resume its full role in GAA competitions when the internment camps finally opened and the amalgamation of the pro and anti treaty players produced their strongest teams.

As Marcus de Burca confirmed:

"It then became apparent that the camaraderie that had grown up behind prison bars provided a firm foundation for Kerry's astonishing run of successes on the football field in the late 1920s." [1]

However, it had been a long wait for Kerry through the bleak years from 1914 to 1925, the latter being the year they won the 1924 All Ireland Final. It was only Kerry's sixth All Ireland title.

Interest in the game had taken a back seat to Volunteer activities. Headed by Austin Stack, many of the rank and file of the Volunteer force were GAA players and supporters and so game fixtures and organisation suffered as a result. The pressures on GAA competitions in Kerry began when the Volunteers received such strong support from rank and file GAA members at the inaugural mass meeting held in Tralee in December 1913.

Papers collected from that time, and a synopsis compiled by the late Mícheál O'Rourke, President of the Kerry GAA until his death at 84 in 1994, show the turbulence of those times in Kerry. It outlines the confusion and lack of organisation in Kerry football at that period, with its leaders more than busy with their political activities. The games suffered and quite a deal of unrest and in-fighting at committee level in Kerry was evident. [2]

After many years of agitation it had seemed that Ireland was about to be granted Home Rule. The Ulster Unionists, however, wanted no part of it, so in January 1913 the Ulster Volunteer

Force was formed. On November 1st, 1913 an article appeared in 'An Claidheamh Solais', entitled "The North Began". Written by Professor Eoin Mac Neill, the article suggested that the other counties in Ireland should follow the example of those in the North.

Mícheál O'Rourke believed this gave the the I.R.B. a great opportunity to further their cause.[3] In Dublin, an organising committee was formed. Half of its members were I.R.B. (Irish Republican Brotherhood) men. On November 25th,, 1913 they held a public meeting in the Rotunda in Dublin City, and it was at this meeting that the Irish Volunteers were formed. Over 3,000 men enrolled, many of them rank and file members of the GAA.[4] In fact, one of the speakers on the platform was Luke O'Toole, secretary of the Central Council. The Volunteer movement spread rapidly throughout the country.

On December 13th a public meeting to establish a Volunteer Company was held in the County Hall, Tralee. Among those who enlisted was Austin Stack, a member of the I.R.B. since 1910.[5] He and his fellow Republicans took a leading part in spreading the Volunteer movement throughout the county. Stack's position, as Chairman of the Kerry County Board, gave weight and influence to the recruitment drive. In fact, many leading Volunteers were also closely linked with the GAA, e.g. Paddy Cahill, Dick Fitzgerald and Pat (Aeroplane) O'Shea.

The Tralee Company, like those in other parts of the country, put great emphasis on drilling, training in the use of arms and, above all, the holding of parades and marches almost every Sunday. One of the most important of these marches was held in Tralee on June 14th, 1914. The Tralee Volunteers assembled at the County Hall where they were addressed by Fr. Charles Brennan. Later they marched to the Market where they were joined by Volunteer companies from Ardfert, Ballymacelligott, Brosna, Castleisland, Cordal, Currans, Dingle, Knocknagoshel and Ventry. It is estimated that up to 2,000 Volunteers took part in the parade. [6]

A few weeks later the Tralee and Ardfert Company were

reviewed by Padraig Pearse. A glance through 'The Kerryman' for this period shows quite clearly that membership of the Volunteers was spreading to every parish in the county. [7]

The close links between the Volunteer movement and the GAA in Kerry were clearly demonstrated on July 5th when the Tralee Company marched to the railway station to welcome and escort to their hotel the visiting Wexford football team. Many of those who marched were also members of various GAA clubs.

One possible effect on the GAA was the chaotic situation that arose within the county. Playing activity and fixtures suffered drastically. County Championship matches, especially in football, were often postponed or failed to materialise. For instance, the 1914 championship was not completed until January 1916.

The Senior footballers prepared to defend their 1913 All Ireland football title. After defeating Tipperary in the Munster Final, Kerry beat Roscommon and so qualified for the All Ireland Final. Again, Wexford were their opponents. The first game ended in a draw but Kerry succeeded in defeating their rivals in the replay on November 29th, 1914, with the score, 2 goals and 3 points to 6 points. It was the first time that Kerry had successfully defended their title. Carbery wrote in the Christmas edition of the Gaelic Athlete:-

"THEY HAVE EVOLVED A METHOD OF FOOTBALL WHICH IS EVER A PLEASURE TO WATCH AND HAVE BROUGHT THE GAME TO A PITCH OF POPULARITY AND PERFECTION WHICH LOOKED AN IMPOSSIBILITY PRIOR TO THEIR ADVENT. AND THE BEAUTY OF IT ALL IS THAT THEY ARE SPORTSMEN EVERY ONE. NEVER HAVE FOUL, DISHONEST NOR UNGRACEFUL TACTICS BEEN ASSOCIATED WITH THEIR NAME. ON AND OFF THE FIELD THEY BEHAVE THEMSELVES IN A STYLE WHICH DOES CREDIT TO THEIR COUNTY AND THE GAME THEY PLAY." [8]

The team that Carbery spoke about was:- D. FITZGERALD (CAPT); P. HEALY; C. MURPHY; D. DOYLE; P. BREEN; J. SKINNER; J. MAHONY; D. MULLINS; T. COSTELLOE; M. MCCARTHY; J. LAWLOR; C. CLIFFORD; T. RICE; J. RICE; AND P. O'SHEA.

The thousands of people who flocked to Croke Park on that November Sunday could not but be aware of the distant drums of World War One. On August 1st most of Europe had gone to war. Many expected that it would be over in a short time. Little did they realise that it would be a long and bloody war unlike any witnessed up to then. Thousands of Irishmen, including a great many Kerrymen, went to the trenches as cannon fodder, for various reasons, for the British Empire. Some went to escape the dreadful poverty, some on taking Redmond's advice that fighting for Britain would lead to Home Rule. Others, like the great Cork IRA freedom fighter, Commandant General Tom Barry, went for the sheer hell of it.

As Barry related in his personal account of the War of Independence:

"IN JUNE 1915, IN MY SEVENTEENTH YEAR, I HAD DECIDED TO SEE WHAT THIS GREAT WAR WAS LIKE. I CANNOT PLEAD I WENT ON THE ADVICE OF JOHN REDMOND OR ANY OTHER POLITICIAN, THAT IF WE FOUGHT FOR THE BRITISH WE WOULD SECURE HOME RULE FOR IRELAND, NOR CAN I SAY I UNDERSTOOD WHAT HOME RULE MEANT. I WAS NOT INFLUENCED BY THE LURID APPEAL TO FIGHT TO SAVE BELGIUM OR SMALL NATIONS. I KNEW NOTH-ING ABOUT NATIONS LARGE OR SMALL. I WENT TO WAR FOR NO OTHER REA-SON THAN THAT I WANTED TO SEE WHAT WAR WAS LIKE, TO GET A GUN, TO SEE NEW COUNTRIES AND TO FEEL A GROWN MAN." [9]

The English poet Wilfred Owen captured the awful hope-lessness of the conflict:-

What passing-bells for these who die as cattle?
Only the monstrous anger of the guns.
Only the stuttering rifles' rapid rattle can patter out
their hasty orisons.
No mockeries now for them; no prayers nor bells.
Nor any voices of mourning save the choirs,
The shrill, demented choirs of wailing shells;
And bugles calling for them from sad shires.

The young Barry returned safely from the trenches and having heard of the executions of the leaders of the 1916 Rising, was to turn his gun against the British Empire to unequalled effect in the history of the guerilla war against the British.

However, almost 50,000 other Irishmen did not escape this terrible slaughter of World War One. In a speech delivered at Woodenbridge, Co. Wicklow on September 20th, John Redmond called on the Irish Volunteers to fight alongside the British army against Germany and her allies. A split developed in the Volunteer movement. The majority followed Redmond and became known as the National Volunteers. Many of these would "die as cattle" on the fields of Flanders.

A smaller group led by Eoin Mac Neill, consisting of the more extreme nationalists, rejected Redmond's suggestion. They retained the name Irish Volunteer. In Kerry the Volunteers, for the most part, declared for Mac Neill, with Austin Stack coming more and more into prominence. In September 1915 he was appointed brigadier over the Kerry Volunteers by Padraig Pearse, who confided in him that a Rising was planned. Most of Stack's time would now be taken up preparing for that event.

Meanwhile, activity on the G.A.A. fields of Kerry was declining and in many instances it was in a shambles. Although Austin Stack was Chairman of the County Board, his nationalist activities curtailed his involvement in the GAA. Apathy soon set in. Several meetings had to be postponed because of the lack of a quorum. The County Championships were badly neglected. The senior footballers reached the All Ireland Final but were beaten by a brilliant Wexford side. It would be many years before Kerry would again play in Croke Park.

In his poem 'The Fool', Padraig Pearse wrote:-

O wise man, riddle me this: what if the dream come true?
What if the dream come true? and if millions unborn shall
dwell
In the house that I shaped in my heart,
The noble house of my thought? [10]

As the early months of 1916 passed, there was an air of expectancy about. Was Pearse's dream about to be realised? The Volunteers were more visible. By the early spring, the Kerry Volunteers had reached a very high level of training. The British Government had responded by arresting a number of volunteers, amongst whom were some prominent G.A.A. personalities.

The bad attendance at County Board meetings was responsible for the poor state of Gaelic games during these early months of 1916. At the April Board meeting only three members attended.

The Kerryman newspaper carried a stinging attack. It may have been placing football before politics. Anyway, while it seemed to be oblivious to, or anti the political involvement of many leading GAA officials. It still sharply criticised the absent members in the following words:-

"HOW LONG ARE THE GAELS OF THE COUNTY GOING TO STAND THIS KIND OF HUMBUG...WHEN THEY ARE APPOINTING REPRESENTATIVES ON THE COUNTY BOARD FOR THE COMING YEAR, IT IS TO BE HOPED THAT THEY WILL BEAR IN MIND THE RECORDS OF THE MEN WHO WERE 'TOO BUSY TO ATTEND' THE MEETINGS OF THE GOVERNING BODY AND WHO CONVENIENTLY SIDE-TRACKED THE INTERESTS OF THEIR CLUBS WHEN IT, IN ANY WAY, INTERFERED WITH THEIR OWN PERSONAL CONVENIENCE...WHAT THE ASSOCIATION WANTS IS WORKERS NOT MAKE BELIEVERS. THERE IS NO USE IN SENDING FORWARD FIGURE HEADS OR 'DUMMIES'; WE HAVE HAD ENOUGH OF THEM IN THE NOW NEARLY DEFUNCT BODY." [11]

Within a few days of that attack in The Kerryman, events were to happen that would change the course of Irish history. The dream that Pearse wrote of, the Rising that he had spoken about to Stack, was to happen. The planned Rising was fixed for Easter Sunday. Stack had instructed the Volunteers from Tralee and outlying districts to mobilise at the Rink on Easter Sunday at 11 am. The Volunteers themselves had no inkling of the real purpose behind this exercise. Stack was well aware of the extensive British intelligence network. Other Volunteer corps were also alerted. Plans, however, went badly wrong. The Aud, which was to supply guns and ammunition for the Rising, was captured by a British naval vessel. When Mac Neill became aware of the hopelessness of the situation he cancelled all Volunteer parades for Easter Sunday. However, on Monday, April 24th, Pearse led his company of Volunteers to the G.P.O. in O'Connell Street. The Easter Rising had begun, but within a week it had been crushed.

Meanwhile Austin Stack had been arrested. As the week went by several hundred Volunteers were arrested in Kerry, including several GAA players. Many of these were jailed in England and Wales, particularly in Frongoch, where according to Sean O'Mahony's extensive account, there were 37 Kerrymen in the Welsh camp, 15 from Tralee. [12] It was in this prison camp that Kerry and Louth renewed old football rivalries. A Kerry team picked from amongst the prisoners played a Louth team of prisoners. The Kerry team was captained by Dick Fitzgerald and included Billy Mullins, Paddy Cahill and Jimmy Wall. The result was a Kerry victory. Incidentally, Billy Mullins was the man who carried the message from Austin Stack to Padraig Pearse about the ill fated German arms landing, which had been planned for Fenit, Co Kerry.

If there was football being played in the prison camps it did little for the game in Kerry. Victories in prisoner of war camps in Wales did not solve the football problems at home. Matters were going from bad to worse. The last straw came in July, when the Kerry County Board announced that it was withdrawing from the Senior and Junior All Ireland football Championships. It was a decision that shocked the GAA world. Although the apathy prevalent amongst members of the County Board was in part to blame, the fact of the matter was that the County Board was broke.

Over the years Kerry had contested many All Ireland Finals - 1910 against Louth; in 1913 there were the two Croke Memorial matches and later that year the All Ireland Final; in

1914 they were involved in the Final against Wexford and again the following year. Preparations for all these matches had cost money. On each occasion the County Board had to go cap in hand to the public for support. Yet, what was collected was not enough. The result was that the County Board found itself getting deeper and deeper into debt. The subvention from the Central Council wasn't worth talking about. The Kerryman stated:-

"IN THE FIVE GATES ALONE OF THE FIVE FINALS WE TOOK PART IN, THE CENTRAL COUNCIL HANDLED AS FAR AS WE CAN REMEMBER £4,339, BESIDES THE PROVINCIAL GAMES, WHILE ALL WE COST THEM, OUTSIDE THE £75 TRAINING EXPENSES, WERE OUR TICKETS TO DUBLIN AND OUR HOTEL 'KEEP' FROM SUNDAY EVENING TO MONDAY MORNING. SUCH, THEN, WAS THE STATE WE FOUND OURSELVES IN, IN THE JULY OF THIS YEAR (1916). COUNTY CHAMPIONSHIP MATCHES, WITH THE EXCEPTION OF KILLARNEY V TRALEE, DO NOT PAY. OUR COUNTY BOARD HAS NOTHING. IN A NUT-SHELL WE OWE ALL AROUND US DEBTS THROUGH ALL IRELAND TRAINING." [13]

It was an uphill battle. Fortunately for Kerry the new County Board, which was elected in August, appointed Den Joe Baily, as honorary secretary. It is no exaggeration to say that Kerry owes more to him than any other man. He was a most able administrator. By nature he was a conciliator and on many occasions helped cool passions. He succeeded in getting the County Championships restarted and he set about rectifying the financial situation. The main object, for the present, was to keep the games and some interest alive.

At the County Convention, which was held in March 1918, there was still strong opposition to Kerry's participation in the All Ireland football and hurling championships until all outstanding debts were cleared. Eventually it was decided to affiliate and a selection committee was appointed. To help clear the debt, the Central Council granted the County Board £100 while a number of challenge matches were arranged against Louth and Wexford, the proceeds of which were to be given to Kerry.

In August Kerry beat Clare in the football championship but lost to Clare in hurling. However, Tipperary proved too strong for a depleted Kerry team when they met in September.

On November 11th the First World War came to an end. This was followed by a general election in Britain and Ireland. Sinn Fein candidates stood for election. They pledged that if elected they would not take their seats at Westminster, instead they would set up an independent Irish Parliament. Sinn Fein achieved a landslide victory, winning 73 seats as against 26 Unionists and 6 Nationalists. One of the Sinn Fein candidates elected was Austin Stack.

As Tom Barry wrote:

"The rising of 1916 was a challenge in arms by a minority. This (War of Independence) was a challenge by a lawfully established government elected by a great majority of the people. The National and the Alien governments could not function side by side and one had to be destroyed." [14]

As a consequence, 1919 opened with the first official shots of the War of Independence. The killing of two RIC men, Constables James McDonnell from Mayo, and Patrick O'Connell from Cork, by a unit led by Dan Breen and Sean Treacy, at Soloheadbeg in Co. Tipperary is recognised as the first official action of the War. However, in Kerry many claim the raid led by Tom McEllistrim on the Gortatlea RIC Barracks on April 13th, 1918 was the first organised action of the War. Volunteers Richard Laide and John Browne lost their lives as a result of that action. [15]

The War of Independence had begun. On January 21st, Dail Eireann met for the first time in the Mansion House, Dublin. A hundred miles or so away, at Soloheadbeg, a party of Volunteers, including Breen and Treacy, ambushed a cart load of gelignite and shot dead the two R.I.C. men who were escorting it. The next two and a half years were difficult years throughout the country and Kerry was no exception. Although both football and hurling continued to a very restricted degree throughout 1919.

As was the pattern so often in the past, the Kerry Senior hurlers were beaten in the first round of the Championship. In football, Kerry defeated Clare in the Munster Final. They met Galway in the All Ireland Semi-Final. The game ended in a draw but in the replay Galway won with a score of 4 goals and 2 points to 2 goals and 2 points. [16]

The County Championship for 1919 got underway, though late in the year, as the 1918 games had dragged on into the following year. Football was almost dead in Kerry. According to 96 year old IRA man Dan Bally Keating in 1997:

"Had it not been for the inauguration of the Tralee Town League in 1917 and 1918 by local street leaders Donncadha O'Donoghue, Christy Barrett, Thomas O'Regan, Frank Houlihan and Jack McMahon, the revival of football in Kerry might never have come about. When Tralee began the movement, then the rest of Kerry followed. [17] "A new competition was started with the introduction of the North Kerry football League. It was to prove highly successful. One reporter said of it at the time; "Never did the game flourish as it does today." [18]

At the County Convention held on February 14th, 1920, Austin Stack was re-elected Chairman, D.J. Baily, honorary secretary, John Moran and Con Clifford joint treasurers. Although the County Board was still in debt, the figure had been greatly reduced. Cork defeated Kerry that year, bringing the wrath of P.J. O'Connell, vice-chairman of the County Board, down on the players' heads. "I can only come to the conclusion that they are a pack of cripples fit to play only with a team of old age pensioners." [19]

That match was the last game seen on the playing fields of Kerry for twelve months. The Black and Tans had arrived in Ireland in March. They were followed by the Auxiliaries. Terence MacSwiney died on hunger strike on October 25th; Kevin Barry was hanged on November 1st and on November 21st, 1920 - Bloody Sunday - thirteen people were killed and sixty were wounded by the Tans when they opened fire on players and spectators as they watched Tipperary play Dublin in a Gaelic football match in Croke Park. The dead included Michael Hogan, of the Tipperary team. This was in reprisal for the shooting dead of 19 British forces' personnel including 11 Intelligence Agents, 2 Auxiliary Cadets, and one Veterinary Corps Officer by Michael Collins' "Squad" and other IRA men. [20]

The Auxiliaries arrived in Kerry in November. A reign of terror followed. In December, General Macready placed Kerry under martial law. Curfew was imposed from 9 pm to 6 am. A bloody war between the IRA and the Crown Forces engulfed Kerry. The IRA carried out ambushes throughout the county. The Crown Forces retaliated by burning houses in Ballylongford, Listowel and Ballyheigue to mention just a few, as no town or village escaped their terror. The only "law" was the law of the gun.

In January of 1921, District Inspector O'Sullivan was killed in Listowel, by an IRA unit of three men which included Con Brosnan. [21] While the Anglo-Irish Truce was imminent a heavy toll was further registered against the British occupation in the county. During the months of May and June the British lost key officers in Kerry. Major MacKinnon, a commander of the Auxiliaries in the infamous Tralee H.Q., was shot dead by Connie Healy who was an ex British Army man from the town. Future Kerry goalkeeper, Johnny O'Riordan (winner of 3 All Ireland medals) together with two other Boherbee men, Jackie Mason and Tommy Barrett, (later Waldorf Astoria, New York). made up the IRA unit. [22] In the same month, while buying a packet of cigarettes in a shop in Pembroke Street, Head Constable Benson RIC was shot dead by Tommy O'Driscoll. [23]

These three shootings in those horrific times in Kerry are inextricably linked with some of the main characters in this book. In later years they would become household names in the history of Kerry football. This will become clearer in their profiles contained in chapter four.

The killing of MacKinnon in April and Benson in May brought about the most shocking reprisals in the town of

Tralee. Many houses were burned by the British forces and people were shot dead after curfew going about there normal business, including a Mrs Conway who was shot dead on Friday 6th of May as she peered over a half door with her six week old baby Michael in her arms. Mrs Conway, nee Nora Dineen, was the thirty four year old wife of, Engine Driver, Paddy Fox Conway and they lived at 24 Upper Caherina, in the Strand Road area of the town. A man on the run had raced through the house to avoid capture and trying to save the IRA man, when Mrs Conway looked out to check where the Black and Tans were, one of them who was positioned at Caherina Cottages, some distance away, shot her dead.[24]

An aside to the tragic killing of Mrs Conway was the fact that her husband, Paddy, together with a man named Paddy Bolger O'Donoghue, both of whom worked in the Tralee railway, had smuggled Robert Monteith from Spicers to safe passage out of town in Easter Week, 1916. [25] Monteith had accompanied Roger Casement on the ill fated trip on the U-Boat from Germany. Even though suggested locally, it is doubtful if this incident and Mrs Conway's killing were linked.

The last major Kerry action of the War of Independence saw one of the heaviest tolls inflicted on the British forces in the Anglo Irish War in the county when a party of IRA Volunteers ambushed a cycle patrol of Black and Tans and RIC at Castlemaine. [26] Amongst the Volunteers on that day were a number of men who would become prominent in the Kerry GAA in the years to follow, all of whom took the anti-Treaty side in the Civil War.

A graphic account of the action is related by local veteran of the War of Independence, Dan Bally Keating who is now 97 years old.

"It was a hot and cloudless first day of June 1921. At around 11 a.m. word was brought to Dan Mulvihill, adjutant of the local battalion of the Republican forces, that a cycling party of nine Black and Tans, led by a District Inspector, had passed through Castlemaine on their way to Tralee. These Black and

Tans were members of a detachment stationed in Killorglin and were on their way to Tralee to collect pay for the garrison. As it was well known that they would return home that evening, it was immediately decided to ambush them on their way back.

Orders were sent out to members of the battalion in the area and eighteen men were assembled near Castlemaine. Their weapons consisted of one Lee Enfield rifle, one police carbine and shotguns loaded with buck-shot. The site of the ambush was then selected, a half mile long straight stretch of the road where Corcoran's and Galvin's cottages now stand, halfway between Milltown and Castlemaine. It was decided to position the shotgun men at roughly ten yard intervals from cottage to cottage on the left hand ditch. The men with the Lee Enfield and the carbine were to be stationed at the end of the ambush position. When the leader of the Black and Tan party approached the cottage the riflemen were to open fire. This, in turn, would be a signal to the shotgun men to begin shooting.

Earlier in the day, the Castlemaine company enlisted all available help. Between Tralee and Castlemaine was a winding mountain road and to warn of the enemy approach, scouts were posted on both flanks. With these ambush positions and security measures in place the IRA were ready to wipe out the Tans. However, when planning the ambush it was realised they hadn't enough riflemen. To solve this problem Dan Mulvihill sent a messenger to Keel to enlist help and a message was also sent to the "Hut".

The Hut was a hideout in the mountain behind Keel/ Castledrum on the road between Castlemaine and Inch. It was generally used by men on the run and on that June day contained a number of prominent Tralee IRA men who were members of Kerry No 1 Brigade IRA. For various reasons they could not go home as they were on a wanted list.

The Keel company came to Castlemaine immediately and between 2 and 2.30 pm they got into positions. They were inspected by Tom O'Connor, Dan Mulvihill, and O/C Jack Flynn, who later went on to become a Fianna Fail T.D. and represent South Kerry in the Dail.

After about an hour of waiting came the news. William Keane of the Castlemaine Company, whose mission it was to keep ahead of the Tans party, signalled that the cycle party was approaching Castlemaine. The are reported to have stopped on Castlemaine railway bridge suspicious of activity around them.

Meanwhile, under the command of Tadhg Brosnan of Castlegregory, a group of riflemen from the "Hut" had arrived. A number of them under Brosnan went towards the start of the ambush while the rest were stationed at a cottage. Now instead of a carbine and one rifle they had five extra rifles carried by Paddy Paul Fitzgerald, Mike O'Leary, Big Dan O'Sullivan, Donncadha O'Donoghue, Jerry O'Connor, Eugene Hogan and Jerry Myles, all from the "Hut".

The head of the Tans cycling party appeared around the bend. They passed the first cottage cycling steadily, and as the last of the party passed the first cottage the guns opened fire. The District Inspector and two Tans were killed instantly. The sergeant who was travelling directly behind the District Inspector somehow escaped - only momentarily, however, as Jerry O'Connor dispatched a grenade and the sergeant died instantly. The battle was short and intense. All guns were now blazing by the IRA and though the Tans managed to return fire their cause was hopeless as they were caught between two gun fires. In the heat of the battle, two of them managed to escape by crossing a ditch and making for a nearby railway line discarding their tunics and ammunition. They were the only two to escape - their escape made easier by the fact that the other side of the road was not manned by the IRA in case their own people got caught in the crossfire.

The only IRA casualty incurred by the ambush party happened when all gunfire had ceased and the ambush was as good as over. Jerry Myles stood up to survey the situation. A Tan who had stayed hiding in a deep gully in the ditch during the gunfire, also stood up. He spotted Myles and fired. With instant reflex action Myles ducked and the bullet entered at the back of his neck and travelled down his back inflicting a serious wound. The Tan then ran along the ditch towards the bohereen where the IRA were waiting and shot him dead. Jerry Myles was taken to a nearby cottage and his wounds were treated by Dr Sheehan, the Battalion Medical Officer. He was laid on a stretcher of two mattresses placed on a kitchen door and with the help of scouts taken to a safe house in Beaufort, where he stayed overnight and next day he was moved to another safe house in Glencar where, for three months, he was nursed back to complete health by Battalion Nurse, Mary O'Brien." [27]

According to statistics of all the ambushes in Kerry during the War Of Independence, Castlemaine was one of the most devastating to the occupying forces.[28] When the ambush site was cleared the IRA found themselves in possession of eight rifles, six Webley Revolvers, 800 rounds of ammunition, two tunics, and nine new bicycles. All of theses were important supplies for the ongoing fight.

As a youngster in the 1950s, and later as member of the Roger Casement Branch of Fianna Fail in Tralee I got to know many of the Tralee men involved in that ambush. I often contemplated in silence what they had been through and how little they ever spoke about their experiences.

They impressed me as most honourable and disciplined men in both their public and private lives. They had a very unique sense of pride in their country and county. I would always enjoy a chat with one veteran in particular, Paddy Paul Fitzgerald, about football or politics, on which subjects he was most knowledgeable and entertaining. He was a very successful Chairman of Strand Street, Kerins' O'Rahilly's GAA Club during their great run in the mid fifties. He was arrested on the day of "Landing" at Fenit and was imprisoned for the remainder of the Civil War. My father and Paddy Paul were lifelong friends. Paddy Paul outlived Joe by a quarter of a century.

Of the others from Tralee who took part in the Castlemaine ambush, Mike O'Leary stayed a strong Republican all his life and worked in the Tralee Labour Exchange. Big Dan O'Sullivan lived on in Tralee and his grandson, Garry Fernane, was a loyal member and mentor of the Austin Stack's GAA Club, Rock Street, Tralee.

Donncadha O'Donoghue played football for Kerry and lined out in the historic Internees v Kerry game in 1924, but died before my time. Jerry Myles became secretary of the Kerry County GAA Board. A brother of his, Billy, who was also at Castlemaine, died in action during the Civil War. Another member of the ambush party, Eugene Hogan married a sister of Dan Spring T.D., the father of Dick Spring. Hogan's son Gerard still runs the family undertaking business in Tralee. Michael "Forker" McMahon worked in Kellihers Merchants, Tralee. He lived on in the town until his death, as did one of the leaders, Jerry Unkey O'Connor.

The full list of 18 IRA men who took an active part in the Castlemaine ambush were Jerry Unkey O'Connor, Paddy Paul Fitzgerald, Joe Sugrue, Big Dan O'Sullivan, Tadgh Brosnan, John L O'Sullivan, Jerry Cronin, John O'Sullivan, Tom O'Connor, Jack Flynn, Michael McMahon, Mike O'Leary, Billy Myles, Jerry Myles, Eugene Hogan, Dan Mulvihill, Donncadha O'Donoghue and Dan Jeffers. [29]

Amongst those of the RIC/ Black and Tan patrol to lose their lives at Castlemaine were: District Inspector Michael Francis McCaughey from Down, aged 29; Sergeant James Colleary from Sligo, aged 45; Constable Joseph Cooney from Roscommon, aged 25; Constable John S McCormack from Leitrim, aged 20; Constable John Quirke from Cork, aged 33. [30]

In all 38 RIC men lost their lives in Kerry during the War of Independence. Of the 457 RIC men killed in Ireland during the Troubles from 1916 to 1922 there were 96 killed in Cork, 43 in Tipperary, 38 in Limerick, 35 in Kerry, 35 in Clare and 32 in Dublin, 21 in Mayo. [31]

A major effect of the War of Independence in Kerry was to whip up support for the IRA for decades to come, contributing to rigid anti treaty attitudes and the horror of the Civil war that was to follow shortly afterwards.

In July 1921, both sides were war-weary. So, on July 11th the Anglo-Irish truce brought peace to Kerry, if only for a while. People began to pick up the pieces again. The treaty was signed on December 6th and formally ratified by the Dail on January 7th, 1922. Dark clouds of Civil War were looming on the horizon - as brother would fight against brother.

According to John Joe Sheehy, the transition in Kerry from British rule after the War Of Independence was a complex time. It was a difficult period.[32] It seems when the Truce came there was a great feeling of euphoria but the following weeks were tense. Sheehy's unit was out and well prepared. They wanted to see that the Tans behaved themselves. The Tans did not come out, instead the regular military patrolled that night. The people of Tralee might have favoured the Treaty but the followers of Austin Stack managed to secure the town so that it stayed anti-Treaty. There were seven hundred in jail from the Civil War. This was also a time of revenge and burnings of landlord property and of many Big Houses. Lady Fingall described her feelings as her husband and herself sat fully clothed through the night awaiting the burning party to arrive at their home in County Dublin:

"I KEPT MYSELF WARM THROUGH THE COLD HOURS OF DARKNESS...WHILE FINGALL SLEPT, AND I STAYED AWAKE, WAITING FOR THE BURNING PARTY. WE WAITED ALL NIGHT. BUT THEY NEVER CAME. THEY BURNED A SMALL PLACE ON THE WAY AND THEN, PERHAPS, HAD HAD ENOUGH OF IT, AND KILLEEN CERTAINLY, WOULD TAKE A BIT OF DOING. AND PERHAPS THEY WERE WEARY. FOR THE COLD DAWN BROKE ON FINGALL AND MYSELF SITTING SHIVERING IN THE STUDY, WITH THE FIRE GOING TO ASHES, I IN MY FUR COAT WITH MY JEWEL-CASE ON MY KNEES....PRESENTLY WE PULLED THE SHUTTERS BACK AND THE STUDY WAS GREY AND CHILLY IN THE MORNING LIGHT. "THEY WON'T COME NOW." AND WE CLIMBED WEARILY UP THE GREAT STAIRCASE TO BED." [33]

In Kerry, many of the big houses were in ruins after this period. Near Tralee the big houses in Ardfert and Ballyheigue were victims of the burning party. The experiences of the people under the Crosby family as landlords had left an almost indelible bad memory. This was, possibly, partly erased by the destruction of the symbol of their dominance and exploitation of the poor people. Little, if any effective law prevailed and many took their own interpretation of law into their hands. This was the period John Joe Sheehy described as being very difficult.

After the War of Independence, the games still suffered in Kerry. It was almost a year before serious attempts were made to get the games underway again as the Civil War intervened. The 1920 Semi-Final which, owing to the war with Britain, was held up for almost two years, was played. At the County Board meeting held on May 23rd, 1922, the draws were made for the hurling and football championships. However, there was an air of unreality about it all. Even though a general election was held on June 16th, anarchy and war was looming nearer every day.

The Civil War began on June 28th, 1922. Kerry was again placed under martial law. Football, hurling and field sports were, for all practical purposes, non-existant. Supporters of the G.A.A. were found on both sides of the divide; players likewise. On May 24th, 1923, the Civil War ended. During those 11 months Kerry suffered more than any other county from the horrors of the strife. The War left a legacy of great bitterness. People despaired at the damage being done to the people of the county. They wondered could the divisions ever be healed.

In terms of Kerry football and hurling the question remained could those who had worn the Green and Gold with such distinction in the past come together, shake hands and win further honour and glory for Kerry? Would the G.A.A. be the catalyst that would help to heal the deep wounds of division?

Mícheál O'Rourke said:

"Any GAA follower looking in from the outside at that stage must surely have despaired. They could not possibly foresee the healing of the terrible wounds. This healing for which the GAA could proudly take full responsibility." [34]

After the Civil War ended in May 1923, the Government called a general election in August. In Kerry it was fought out between those who favoured the Treaty and those who opposed it. When the results in Kerry were announced, the people had elected four anti-Treaty candidates and three Government candidates. Amongst the former was Austin Stack, President of the Kerry County Board. He was, at that time, in Arbour Hill Jail. The Government gradually freed most of the internees who had fought on the anti-Treaty side. Amongst the Kerrymen who were freed were many notable footballers. While in detention they had played a prominent part in Gaelic games.

An article in The Kerryman on December 27th, 1923:-

"FOR THE PAST FEW WEEKS I HAVE BEEN HEARING FLATTERING REPORTS OF THE VARIOUS INTERNEES AND THE PROMINENT PART TAKEN BY KERRYMEN IN THE FURTHERANCE OF OUR NATIONAL PASTIMES. I HAVE HEARD THAT IN THE VARIOUS TOURNAMENTS, KERRYMEN WERE THE STARS BEATING ALL BEFORE THEM AND WINNING HANDSOMELY IN THE DIFFERENT COMPETITIONS. NOW THAT THE CAMPS ARE BROKEN UP AND THE MAJORITY OF THE FOOTBALLERS AT HOME ONCE AGAIN THERE IS SOME TALK ABOUT THEIR EAGERNESS TO PLAY THIS YEAR'S MUNSTER CHAMPIONS." [35]

In October of that year a make-shift Kerry team had surprised all, even their own supporters, by beating Tipperary in the Munster Final. It was to this team that the Ex-Internees issued a challenge. The game was fixed for February 10th, 1924. It was awaited with great anticipation. Both teams trained as if for a Final. The Kerryman correspondent wrote:-

"EVERY-DAY DURING THE PAST WEEK, THE THUD OF A FOOTBALL CAN BE HEARD IN THE SPORTSFIELD; AND THE EARLY MORNING HOURS ARE DEVOTED TO WALKING EXERCISES...IT WILL BE ADMITTED THAT THE EX-INTERNEES ARE FULLY DETERMINED TO PULL THE LAURELS FROM THE BROWS OF THE KERRY TEAM. ACCOUNTS TO HAND FROM THE LATTER, POINT TO THE FACT THAT THE

MAJORITY OF THEM ARE PUTTING IN SOME USEFUL WORK. THEY ARE GOING THROUGH A SOMEWHAT SIMILAR COURSE OF TRAINING AS THAT WHICH PRE-CEDED THE MUNSTER FINAL." [36]

It was a match between the experienced Kerry team and the youthful team of ex-internees. Unfortunately the heavy rain had left the pitch sodden. The game itself "...was robust at times rather too much and from start to finish was keenly contested." At the final whistle the Kerry team had won with the score 5 points to 1 point. The teams were:-

KERRY: D. HURLEY; TOM RYLE; TOM O'CONNOR; PHIL O'SULLIVAN; JACK SHEEHY; TOM KELLIHER; D. O'CONNOR (KILLARNEY); CON BROSNAN; DONNCADHA O'DONOGHUE; TOM MAHONY; M. WALSH (PAWTACK) FROM MOYVANE; P. MURPHY; M. GRAHAM (DINGLE); P. DONOVAN (KILLARNEY) AND JIMMY BAILY.

EX-INTERNEES: JOHN O'RIORDAN; JERRY (PLUGGY) MORIARTY; JOE BARRETT; BILL O'GORMAN; EUGENE MORIARTY (KILLARNEY); JOE MacMAHON (FARMERS BRIDGE); JOHNNY TANGNEY (RACECOURSE ROAD, TRALEE); DENIS MAHONY (CURROW); T. O'DONNELL; JACKIE RYAN; BUDDLE SHEEHY (BOHERBEE , TRALEE); C. CRONIN; J. MURPHY; MAURICE MAHER (BOHERBEE, TRALEE); P. DALY. [37]

(Not all the Christian names are available today, Dan Bally Keating supplied a number of Christian names which had evaded Mícheál O'Rourke and others).

A return match was fixed for March 23rd. This time the Ex-Internees turned the tables with a decisive win over the Kerry team. This match was played in a most sporting spirit. It augured well for the future. When the selectors met to pick the team to play Cavan in the All Ireland Semi-Final, they were determined to pick the best from both sides. This resulting team became a great unifying force in the county. It became the focal point for Kerry people. They could identify with it. They were at one when it came to the honour and glory of the county. The footballers knew that they bore a heavy responsibility. If any member of the team was asked why he buried all previous rancour and bitterness, perhaps, he would echo the words of another great Kerry footballer and say, "We did it for Kerry." [38] It was a sentiment that would be severely tested within a few weeks.

On 27th April, 1924, Kerry met Cavan in the All Ireland football Semi-Final. It had been nine years since Kerry had last played in Croke Park. In the intervening years Ireland had "changed utterly." [39] Kerry people had experienced great suffering and hardship. The appearance of this Kerry team at Croke Park had more than usual significance. Let us first allow The Kerryman reporter to take up the story:-

"CAVAN, IN ROYAL BLUE, WERE FIRST UPON THE FIELD. THEY WERE WARMLY RECEIVED. IT WAS EVIDENT THAT THEIR FOLLOWERS NUMBERED THOUSANDS AND THEY MADE NO SECRET OF THE FACT THAT THEY CAME SOUTH TO WIN. SOON A YOUTHFUL BRIGADE IN THEIR EARLY TWENTIES STALKED UPON THE FIELD. ROUND AFTER ROUND OF VOCIFEROUS CHEERING GREETED THEIR APPEARANCE. THEY WERE CLAD IN GREEN AND GOLD AND CAME FROM KERRY. ON ENTERING THE FIELD, THE KERRY TEAM PROCEEDED TO THE SPOT WHERE MICHAEL HOGAN THE TIPPERARY PLAYER WAS SHOT ON 'BLOODY SUNDAY'. THEY KNELT IN PRAYER ON THE FATAL SOD WHILE THE SPECTATORS MAINTAINED A RESPECTFUL SILENCE." [40]

That simple, but profound gesture was not lost on the assembled gathering. Many had taken opposite sides during the Civil War. Some had just come out of Free State Prison Camps but on that day in Croke Park these Kerrymen were brothers again. Their example would not be lost on their county men and women. The healing process had begun - the scars of the Civil War were beginning to heal. The Kerry team on that April Sunday included men who, just a short time before, had fought each other in a bitter war.

Kerry would now meet Dublin in the All Ireland Final on June 15th. Prior to that, however, P.J. Cahill, an anti-Treaty T.D.

for Kerry wrote to The Liberator. In the course of his letter he said:-

"THE PRESIDENT OF THE KERRY COUNTY BOARD, AUSTIN STACK, AND TWO MEMBERS OF THE COUNTY FOOTBALL TEAM, HUMPHREY MURPHY AND MOSS GALVIN, ARE STILL IN PRISON...I SUGGEST THAT THE COUNTY BOARD NOTIFY THE CENTRAL COUNCIL THAT KERRY WILL NOT PLAY THE ALL IRELAND FOOTBALL FINAL UNTIL SUCH TIME AS THE PRESIDENT OF THE KERRY COUNTY BOARD AND HIS FRIENDS ARE RELEASED." [41]

Cahill's proposal was fraught with danger. In the wake of the Civil War and the slender thread that bound the Kerry team together, there was a distinct possibility that old wounds would again be opened. Against that background the members of the Kerry team and the Selection Committee held a meeting at the Ashbourne Hotel on the evening of June 10th. What exactly was said at that meeting was not recorded but we do know that both the team and the Selection Committee took the most crucial decision ever for the G.A.A. in Kerry. They decided that they would not play Dublin until the political prisoners were released. Whatever other consequences there may have been for Kerry, a split was averted and unity maintained. The key figure in the discussion was D.J. Baily, whose contribution to the well-being of the G.A.A. in Kerry was unsurpassed.

Following that meeting, D.J. Baily and John Joe Sheehy went to Dublin to explain Kerry's stand. After listening to the Kerry delegates, however, the Central Council decided to award the Final to Dublin. Kerry were not without their backers. Limerick now refused to travel for the hurling Final until the political prisoners were released. Galway were awarded the Final but refused to accept it. Limerick and Kerry were also suspended. Then at a specially convened Convention, Galway proposed that all suspensions be lifted and the Finals refixed. Austin Stack was released in July and so the way was clear for the Final with Dublin which was refixed for September 28th.

Although, Kerry lost the Final by 1-5 to 1-3, 1924 had been a memorable and historic year for the county. The outlook for the future was brighter.

In October Kerry beat Clare in the 1924 Munster Final; they then went on to beat Mayo. Once again Kerry were in the All Ireland Final and for the second year running, faced Dublin. Excitement gripped the county. P.J. O'Connell, Chairman of the County Board, called on all the players to train hard. With rousing words he urged them to:-

"Train in your own districts, walking, skipping and football practice. Let every man do his part and when the supreme test arrives we will be able as always to hold our own against the cream of Ireland's footballers." [42]

A training fund was launched. Subscriptions poured in from far and near. Whist drives were organised and dances were held in order to raise money. A spirit of pride was felt throughout the county.

As the day of the Final drew near, arrangements were made to convey as many supporters as possible to the game. Six special trains left Kerry carrying almost 4,000 fans. The attendance at the match was 30,000, which broke all previous records. [43] It was a most memorable game, with Kerry winning their first All Ireland Senior title after a lapse of ten years.

One of the Kerry stars was a young clerical student, Mundy Prendeville. It was his final appearance for Kerry as shortly he would be ordained a priest and leave for Perth. He later became a distinguished Archbishop of Perth. A strange footnote to this young Kerryman's football career is the fact that he had been prevented from being ordained in Maynooth College, where he had completed his studies over the previous six years. Prendeville broke the strict rules of that era by climbing the wall of the college to play with Kerry in Croke Park in the All Ireland Final. He paid the penalty by being disallowed from ordination with his his fellow classmates. He was ordained separately at Clonliffe College and was immediately consigned as young priest to a life in Australia, albeit a very successful one. The writer's mother has pleasant memories of Archbishop Prendeville coming to Fenit near Tralee to visit his old team mate, my father, during his illness in the late forties.

The excitement that followed that 1924 All Ireland Final win, though played in April 1925, showed the resurgence of interest was rife. News of the victory was posted on the window of The Kerryman office in Tralee. Wires were sent to New York notifying the Kerrymen's Association of the result. The news was greeted with wild excitement in Celtic Park. Paddy McKenna, Captain of the New York Kerry team, wrote:-

"We all went mad here when we heard the result...Some of us got homesick and thought of home and the scene in Barry's Hotel, Dublin." [44]

Chapter Notes

(1) De Burca, Marcus. The GAA A History. p40.

(2) O'Rourke, Mícheál. Papers.

(3) Ibid.

(4) Ibid.

(5) Ibid.

(6) Ibid.

(7) Ibid.

(8) Carbery Annual 1914.

(9) Barry, Tom. Guerilla Days in Ireland. p2.

(10) Pearse, Padraig. From his poem, The Fool. Quotations of P.H.Pearse. Mac Aonghusa, P.

(11) O'Rourke papers.

(12) O'Mahony, Sean. Frongoch, pp204-205.

(13) O'Rourke papers.

(14) Barry, Tom. Guerilla Days In Ireland. p5.

(15) Dwyer, Ryle. Memoirs of Tom McEllistrim. The Kerryman. August 19th, 1994.

(16) O'Rourke papers.

(17) Ibid.

(18) Interview with Dan Bally Keating 1997.

(19) O'Rourke papers.

(20) Gleeson, James. Bloody Sunday.

(21) Gaughan, Anthony. Listowel and Its Environs, p381.

(22) Mac Eoin, Uinseann. Survivors. p357.

(23) Interview John Joe Landers.

(24) Interview Paddy and Bertie Conway, grandsons of Paddy from his second marriage.

(25) Ibid.

(26) Keating, Dan. Interview 1997, and Kerry's Fighting Story (1947).

(27) Keating, Dan. Interview 1997.

(28) Keating, Dan. Interview and also Kerry's Fighting Story (1947).

(29) Kerry's Fighting Story. Published by The Kerryman 1947.

(30) Herlihy, Jim. The Royal Irish Constabulary. pp154 to 231.

(31) Ibid. p152.

(32) Mac Eoin, Uinseann. Survivors. see John Joe Sheehy p357, 358.

(33) O'Rourke papers.

(34) The Kerryman article, December 27th, 1923.

(35) Seventy Years Young. Elizabeth, Countess of Fingall. Collins, London 1937. pp440, 441.

(36) The Kerryman article, probably January or early February 1924.

(37) O'Rourke papers.

(38) Ibid.

(39) Yeats quote.

(40) O'Rourke papers.

(41) Letter from Tralee Republican, Paddy Cahill, to Kerry newspaper "The Liberator".

(42) O'Rourke papers.

(43) Ibid.

(44) Ibid.

Chapter 4

Tragedies of Kerry

In this chapter I will attempt to ascertain why Kerry above all other counties displayed such calculated ferocity and bitterness during the Civil War. I will try to understand how such outrageous military tactics and behaviour became acceptable and could be justified as acts of war. I will relay to you the situations in which both sides found themselves and the decisions taken which were to have drastic and far reaching effects. In the end, only the reader can decide if any or all of the actions taken were legitimate and necessary or just other examples of man's inhumanity to man.

You will be faced as have so many in the past with the age old question of when, if ever, it is justifiable to take the life of another, and what cause justifies such an action. Each of us will have our own opinions on this dilemma, and our upbringing may colour our sympathies or otherwise. As the reader you will judge for yourself but I urge you to witness the deeds and actions of that generation with compassion and understanding, and perhaps reserve your judgement somewhat, irrespective of your political affiliations.

Since this is a story of reconciliation of a bitterly divided people, to understand the extent and latitude of tolerance shown by both sides, it is therefore essential to coldly recount some of the most unsavoury details from the Civil War in Kerry. This, it is hoped, will help to assess the enormity of the task of social rehabilitation and bridge building which was necessary after the fighting ended.

I would like to stress that such recounting of past atrocities is only necessary to highlight the enormity of the achievement in bringing about such reconciliation. It is worth examining this reconciliation in Kerry to see if it might be fruitfully applied to today's problems in the Six Counties of Northern Ireland, should a lasting peace come about.

I will endeavour to show that the GAA was the main vehicle in uniting the people of Kerry after the Civil War. It provided an opportunity for the people to unite in a common purpose and interest. This achievement in reuniting a war-torn people under the common colour of the Kerry football jersey was remarkable and peculiar to the GAA.

However, when I say that the GAA helped reconcile this bitterness, for my claim to be realistic I must first illustrate the depth of bitterness that existed in Kerry at that time. It appears to me that the bitterness took two forms, both covert and overt. The latter being the form that needed immediate addressing in Kerry for normal life to return after such open hostility. The covert form was to be the kind that the GAA, the six men profiled in this book and that generation of footballers helped to reconcile.

The covert, however, is a more resilient kind of bitterness. It is one that remains private and is usually spoken of in whispers. It tends to be the preserve of the relatives and close friends of the victims and perpetrators of the atrocities. Very often the secrets have been taken to the grave.

Many accounts have been written of the too numerous dastardly deeds perpetrated by both sides. Nobody wins a civil war. For the foul taste of losing or winning passes on through generations for many years. In the book Green Against Green, Michael Hopkinson confirms the unique depth of bitterness present in the Kerry story of the Civil War.

"The conflict in Kerry will always be associated with the atrocious events of March 1923, which left behind a bitterness remarkable even in the context of civil war." [1]

Former Chief of Staff of the IRA and future Minister for External Affairs (1951-4, 1957-9), Frank Aiken was quoted as using the words of an old priest:

"War with the foreigner brings to the fore all that is best and noblest in a nation - Civil War all that is mean and base." [2]

One even doubts this lofty assertion about war per se. Even

from this distance one would have to agree with a veteran of the Japanese/American Pacific War, when he said:

"If the survivors of war were the policy makers there would be no more wars."[3]

The depths to which men dredged during the Civil War in Kerry, if not in Ireland, yielded an even grimmer harvest in savagery and damage to Irish society than that of the preceding War of Independence, for it was to linger and haunt. The British were gone, the Irish had to live with each other.

In Kerry it was at its most terrible. I recall in childhood the bitterness which still lingered in places between families on opposite sides. To totally bring back peace and tolerance to the tattered social fabric was indeed a mammoth task.

The dark deeds of the month of March 1923 in Kerry alone were enough to maintain festering sores for generations. To live with any one of the particular atrocities of that infamous month would test the character of any people. In Kerry, that month left a list of shameful doings, as outrage followed outrage, to leave a shadow on a people which has scarcely faded in some minds, to this day.

That a county could ever unite again under a single flag, not to mind, a football jersey, is a lasting tribute to the people who stood up to be counted in face of great personal physical danger and the risk of intense public opprobrium. Had the uniting force of Gaelic football not been present as a distraction and common bond in the Kingdom in the twenties and thirties, it is debatable as to where the post Civil War years would have led. Clearly the residual bitterness would have lingered for much longer with a significant section of the population.

As it was, it took some outstanding examples of courage to overcome the hatred in families, parishes, villages, towns and GAA clubs. There were people like Con Brosnan of Moyvane who was a potent force in the rehabilitation of County Kerry in the twenties and thirties. For, though holding strong political beliefs, Brosnan never allowed these feelings to interfere with his love for the common affinity in Kerry of Gaelic football.

When the Civil War started, the great majority of Kerry people in 1922 supported the Anti-Treaty lobby. They were prepared to fight in defence of De Valera, but mainly Stack whom they revered. Stack had been, of course, a Minister in the Provisional Government under President De Valera prior to the Treaty. He was thus the major link and influence on the Republican people of the area. They controlled Kerry, or so they thought. They appear not to have fully appreciated the possibility of an amphibious assault on the county by the Free State forces. They were caught off-guard in August when Government troops landed at Fenit, Cahirciveen and Tarbert. The real and dirtiest period of the Civil War was yet to come in the following nine months.

That same month of August 1922 saw Michael Collins shot at Beal na mBlath in County Cork while trying to make peace moves with De Valera, to try to stop the three month old Civil War going any further. The killing of Collins contributed to much greater bitterness and consequently a worsening of the Civil War where it still raged. It was, arguably, the saddest of all the regrettable killings of the Civil War. We lost Ireland's greatest military mind, the architect of the defeat of the British in the War of Independence. The fact that he had survived the best efforts of the British to capture or kill him and then lose his life at the hands of his own people was particularly tragic. However, compounding this tragedy is the belief in some quarters that Eamon de Valera could have participated in the action which led to the death of Ireland's greatest soldier.

A close friend of mine, Sean Quilter of Tralee, now living in the USA was Chaplain to Eamon de Valera when he was President of Ireland from 1959 to 1973. Dev confirmed unequivocally to Sean that his reason for being in West Cork at the same time as Collins was for the express purpose of a peace meeting. The former Fr. Quilter, now married in Florida, told me Dev had a great love for Collins and prayed for him every day of his life.

"SEPTEMBER 1997
FLORIDA
DEAR J J,
GLAD TO HEAR FROM YOU. I AM LOOKING FORWARD TO YOUR BOOK WHICH I KNOW WILL BRING GREATER UNDERSTANDING OF A DIFFICULT PERIOD IN WHICH BOTH OUR FATHERS WERE INVOLVED.

YES I DID HAVE THE PRIVILEGE OF SHARING A GLASS OF GUINNESS OR TWO WITH PRESIDENT DE VALERA IN THE LATE '60S, WITH HIS CLOSE FRIEND LT. COLONEL TOM MCNAMARA OF CRUSHEEN. "THE CHIEF" RARELY TALKED POLITICS, BUT I DO RECALL THAT HE SAID HE WAS IN COUNTY CORK TO BRING ABOUT A TRUCE WHEN MICHAEL COLLINS WAS SHOT. HE PERSONALLY REGRETTED AND TRIED TO AVERT THIS TRAGEDY. IT WAS ONE OF HIS GREATEST PRAYERS AND WISHES TO BRING PEACE AND RECONCILIATION TO ALL IRISH PEOPLE.

I HOPE THIS ANSWERS YOUR QUESTION ALAS, VERY BRIEFLY. WILL WRITE SOON.

SLAN AGUS BEANNACHT,
SEAN QUILTER"[4]

Nobody will ever know whether the atrocities in Kerry would have happened if Michael Collins had survived. Many believe he would never have presided over, or condoned such inhumane treatment of his fellow Irishmen and former comrades. He died in August 1922 and the Civil War took a more terrible turn in the ensuing months, in which March and April of 1923 brought the period known as the Tragedies of Kerry. This was the legacy which the County of Kerry inherited from the differences between Michael Collins and Eamon De Valera over the Treaty with Britain. The blood that was to be spilled so profusely and the hatred generated would only be forgotten eventually when the county united through the support for a football jersey.

Collins was shot on August 22nd at Beal na mBlath, in County Cork. By the time the following month arrived many Kerry Republicans were interned and others were fighting with flying columns in Limerick and Tipperary. But, although the

Kerry towns were firmly under the control of the Free State Army, guerilla warfare in the countryside of the county was growing in intensity. Disruption of normal everyday life was intensifying, with food scarcities, ambushes on army troops and the blowing up of bridges and railway lines.

An extract from this newspaper shows just how bad things had become within the County of Kerry, and still in terms of loss of life the worst was yet to come.

FREEMAN'S JOURNAL 02/09/1922

"FOOD SCARCITY

MILITARY RATION FLOUR SUPPLIES IN KERRY

DISTRESSED AREAS

PEOPLE SUFFER THROUGH WAR ON TRANSPORT

OWING TO THE CAMPAIGN WHICH IS BEING WAGED AGAINST ALL FORMS OF TRANSPORT, CERTAIN AREAS HAVE BEEN REDUCED TO A CONDITION BORDERING ON WANT. SO GRAVE IS THE FOOD SITUATION IN KERRY THAT BRIGADIER GENERAL O'DALY HAS ISSUED THE FOLLOWING REGULATION:"

"AS A STATE OF WAR EXISTS IN THE COUNTRY, I RESERVE THE RIGHT TO POOL ALL FOOD SUPPLIES IN KILLARNEY, UNTIL SUCH TIME AS THE PEOPLE IN THE TOWN NOMINATE A MAN AS FLOUR CONTROLLER. THIS COURSE IS ESSENTIAL OWING TO THE EXTREME SHORTNESS OF FLOUR AND THE THREATENED STARVATION TO THE TOWN'S PEOPLE."

RAILWAY TRAFFIC TO LISTOWEL FROM LIMERICK HAS BEEN RESUMED, AND TRADERS ARE NOW IN A POSITION TO RENEW THEIR BUSINESS WITH DUBLIN. THE TOWN IS STILL CUT OFF FROM CORK BY RAIL.

DURING THE MONTH OF ISOLATION, LISTOWEL WAS VISITED BY AN ECONOMIC PARALYSIS, FROM WHICH IT IS BUT SLOWLY RECOVERING. ALL THE ROADS LEADING TO THE TOWN WERE IMPASSABLE, WITH THE RESULT THAT THERE WAS NO FAIR OR MARKETS. TRADE WAS AT A STANDSTILL AND TO EMPHASISE THE GENERAL STAGNATION, A LOCAL RAILWAY STRIKE TOOK PLACE, SEVERING COMMUNICATION WITH LISSELTON AND BALLYBUNION. AS IN OTHER PARTS OF THE COUNTRY, MANY BRIDGES HAVE BEEN PARTIALLY DESTROYED OR RENDERED WHOLLY USELESS.

BEFORE THE RESUMPTION OF FAIRS AND MARKETS MEANT GREAT LOSSES TO THE AGRICULTURAL COMMUNITY, BUT THE PROSPECTS ARE RELIEVED BY THE CERTAINTY OF A FAIRLY GOOD HARVEST ALL ROUND. HAY, CORN, ROOT CROPS AND POTATOES ARE MUCH BETTER GENERALLY THAN THEY WERE LAST YEAR.

AFTER A LONG PERIOD OF DISUSE, THE MARKET SQUARE AT ABBEYFEALE PRESENTS, IN PART, THE APPEARANCE OF A PASTURE FIELD, BEING COVERED OVER WITH GRASS.

THE MAIN ROAD TO CASTLEISLAND IS CUT BY THE DESTRUCTION OF THE MINOR ARCH AT WELLESLEY BRIDGE, WHICH CONNECTS BROSNA, ROCKCHAPEL AND KNOCKNAGOSHEL WITH ABBEYFEALE. IN CONSEQUENCE OF THIS DISCONNECTION, FARMERS ON THE LIMERICK SIDE OF THE BRIDGE ARE SERIOUSLY HANDICAPPED AS THEY ARE UNABLE TO CART TURF OR SUPPLY THEIR CREAMERY EXCEPT AT VERY GREAT INCONVENIENCE AND RISK. - BRIGADIER GENERAL O'DALY." [5]

Previously, Paddy O'Daly was head of the Active Service Unit in Dublin, which included the Squad, Collins' hand picked IRA men responsible for the killing of the British Intelligence agents on Bloody Sunday, 1920. These men remained loyal to Collins. However, O'Daly's high reputation as a Volunteer in the War of Independence, was seriously damaged as a result of the atrocities in Kerry, for which he mainly took the blame. O'Daly's brother, Frank, who fought on the Republican side in the Civil War, was incarcerated in Portlaoise Prison. A fellow IRA man, Dan Keating, who was in prison with Frank O'Daly in Portlaoise credited Paddy for having saved the lives of Mossy Galvin and Johnny O'Connor when they were to be shot by firing squad in Ballymullen Barracks, Tralee. [6]

When the "Kerry Landing" took place at Fenit on August 2nd, 1922 the invading troops were assisted by local leader Eamon A. Horan. After active involvement in the War of Independence the Tralee man was one of the few from the area who had, in the face of considerable odds, taken the side of

Michael Collins. Other locals who became officers and were known as the Dandy Six were Tom Slattery, Billy Clifford, Stephen Scannell, Jack Flavin, Harold Reid and Jimmy Lyons. Horan was vociferous in his defence of Collins as the Civil War dawned over Kerry. It was Horan who arrested Joe Barrett in Doon, near Tralee and a story recounted about that arrest shows the fairness of Horan's attitude towards his former friends and neighbours. His dilemma as a Tralee man is also borne out by documentation which came into the possession of the author of this book.

It seems that when Barrett and, his eventual brother-in-law, Henry Carrick, were arrested by Free State Officer Horan, a soldier in the arresting party struck Joe Barrett a number of times. Barrett had his hands bound behind him during this treatment and when he verbally challenged the soldier, Horan heard the commotion. A keen boxing follower, and former pugilist himself, the Tralee officer untied Barrett and made a ring. When Joe had got his revenge Horan had him arrested and bound again.[7] Barrett never forgot this favour for Horan and years afterwards, as a child, the author remembers Eamon A Horan and Joe spending many an hour chatting as they took their daily walk around The Green, Town Park in Tralee.

Horan had tried to protect a prisoner named Jack Galvin of Killorglin, who was amongst a group of 20 prisoners arrested after a major battle in the town now famous for Puck Fair. When Horan left him, with a broken arm, in a lorry while going to assist in the removal of a road block, Galvin was taken off the lorry and shot by other officers. [8]

Horan was furious and challenged the Tralee command.

This more serious example of his divided loyalties, between duty to his uniform and the neighbourly welfare of former Tralee friends is documented in a memorandum sent by Comdt. General W.R.E. Murphy. Horan had challenged many of the tactics used by the Dublin Guards officers against local people while trying to take control of Kerry.

"OGLAIGH NA HÉIREANN
G.O.C. DEPARTMENT
FIELD GENERAL HEADQUARTERS,
KERRY COMMAND,
TRALEE, OCTOBER 1ST 1922

TO:
THE COMMANDER IN CHIEF
G.H.Q. DUBLIN
A CHARA,

I APPEND REPORTS FOR THE WEEK ENDING THE 30-9-'22. I WOULD URGENTLY ASK THAT YOU SEND 500 MEN HERE IMMEDIATELY. TREACHERY IS RAMPANT IN KERRY NO. I BRIGADE. THE MEN SELL THEIR AMMUNITION, RECEIVING 12/6 PER BANDOLIER. I HAVE SET TRAPS FOR THEM AND HAVE TAKEN THEM REDHANDED. AN OFFICER WHO WAS EMPLOYED HERE FIRST WROTE TO THE IRREGULAR LEADER CAHILL ASKING HIS PERMISSION TO TAKE ON THE JOB. HE IS EMPLOYED BY THE LOCAL BRIGADIER HORAN. I CANNOT TRUST ANY OFFICER OR MAN OF THE LOT. I ASK YOU VERY URGENTLY TO REMOVE THEM FROM THIS COUNTY AND SEND ME OTHER MEN. IF THIS CANNOT BE DONE I INTEND TO PARADE THE LOT IN FRONT OF THE 1ST WESTERN AND "DANNY BOY" AND SHOOT THEM DOWN. I CANNOT RISK VALUABLE OFFICERS LIVES FOR THESE SCOUNDRELS. IT IS ONLY HOPELESS TO WORK HERE WITH TREACHERY ALL AROUND AND IF NO TRUSTWORTHY MEN CAN BE SENT I RESPECTFULLY ASK YOU TO RECALL ME FROM THIS COMMAND AS I CANNOT CONSCIENTIOUSLY BE RESPONSIBLE FOR MEN'S LIVES UNDER THE CIRCUMSTANCES.

HORAN THE LOCAL LEADER IS KNOCKING UP A ROW ABOUT AN IRREGULAR GALVIN WHO WAS SHOT BY THE 1ST WESTERN. THIS SCOUNDREL SHOT CAPT. BURKE, SIGNED A FORM GOT OUT AND TOOK UP ARMS AGAIN. HE WAS THE TERROR OF THE COUNTRYSIDE. IN ANY CASE I WILL NOT HAVE IT QUESTIONED BY HORAN AND WILL NOT SACRIFICE ANY OFFICER OR MAN OF THE 1ST WESTERN (A SPLENDID LOT OF TROOPS) FOR HIS CHEAP HEROICS. FOR HIS OWN SAFETY HE AND HIS TREACHEROUS COMRADES HAD BEST BE REMOVED. HE IS CLOSELY WATCHED AT PRESENT.

WE ARE FIGHTING HERE AGAINST VERY SUPERIOR FORCES, IN A MAINLY HOSTILE COUNTRY AND CANNOT AFFORD TO OVERLOOK ANYTHING. I CAN

PICK A CERTAIN NUMBER OF RELIABLE MEN OUT OF THE KERRY TROOPS TO KEEP ON AS LOCAL GUIDES. THE REST BETTER BE SENT TO SOME OTHER AREA, WHERE THEY CANNOT SELL THEIR RIFLES OR THEIR POSTS.

THE PEOPLE HERE ARE VERY PLEASED WITH OUR ACTIVITY AND WE CAN GRADUALLY GET SUPPORT BUT ONLY BY SHOWING OURSELVES "TOP DOG". I WILL ASK YOU TO GIVE THIS YOUR IMMEDIATE ATTENTION AND TO SEND ON UNDER RELIABLE OFFICERS A BATCH OF MEN AS SOON AS POSSIBLE. A FEW "ORIEL HOUSE" AGENTS ARE ALSO REQUIRED. WE HAVE NOW 120 PRISONERS HERE AND I WOULD ASK THAT THEY BE REMOVED AS WE HAVE NOT GOT A SUFFICIENT NUMBER OF MEN TO GUARD THEM PROPERLY.

MISE LE MEAS MOR

W.R.E. Murphy

W.R.E. MURPHY
COMDT. GENERAL
G.O.C. KERRY COMMAND" [9]

*Note: "Oriel House", off Merrion Square, Dublin, was the H.Q. of the CID, where Free State agents had a doubtful reputation for alleged torture methods adopted within its walls.

The winter of 1922 saw the troops under Brigadier General O'Daly holding a firm grip on the towns of the county. However, there was still a great deal of fight left in the IRA and its supporters. The Civil War in Kerry was really only beginning.

As Hopkinson put it:

"GENERAL W.R.E. MURPHY'S OPTIMISTIC REMARKS ABOUT HAVING BROKEN THE BACK OF REPUBLICAN RESISTANCE IN KERRY - MADE WHEN HE LEFT THE COMMAND IN JANUARY 1923 - WERE NOT PROVED JUSTIFIED." [10]

By 1923 the Civil War in Kerry had reached a point of stalemate, characterised by few large scale confrontations. There were failed and costly attacks on Castlemaine in January, on

Kenmare in February, and on Cahirciveen in March. Most of the activity could be described in terms of guerilla warfare with raids, the destruction of communications and ambushes being the tactics employed. The Free State troops made large sweeps of IRA territory but were generally unsuccessful. It was not until the end of the war that the south and east of the county were cleared of IRA columns.

The behaviour of the Free State towards prisoners was rumoured to be harsh, sometimes to the extreme. As referred to by Hopkinson, a Free State Army inspection report stressed that Paddy O'Daly's command left a lot to be desired in discipline and behaviour. [11] Niall Harrington, the author of the book Kerry Landing, himself a former Free State Officer stationed in Tralee, confirms as true allegations that improper conduct was practised by some officers in the Free State Army. [12] Summary executions were all too common throughout the country, where 77 Republicans were executed by firing squad between November 1922 and May 1923. Only four of these were by order of the Cabinet, the others were under the special powers held by the army. There were seven executions by firing squad in Ballymullen Barracks, Tralee.

Some would go as far as to say that such unprofessional conduct by the Free State troops actually contributed to the severity of the IRA attacks. Yet on the other hand, the methods used against the Free State Army troops would have tested the discipline and control of any army. The booby-trap mine is an example of one of the most extreme tactics of the IRA.

In Green against Green, Hopkinson said it is difficult to establish proof for many of the crimes attributed to O'Daly's troops. Nevertheless, O'Daly and his officers failed badly to answer the various charges in a satisfactory manner, and little attempt was made by Free State GHQ to deal with the problems. [13]

Harrington gave first hand evidence of witnessing three officers leaving the Tralee army garrison to carry out the shooting of two railway engine drivers. [14] It seemingly was intended, by the Free State officers, to blame the local IRA for the killings.

The Weekly Freeman newspaper of January 27th, 1923 reported the shooting as follows: "While engine drivers Dan Daly and Dan Lynch were chatting on the roadside outside Tralee Railway Station at 7.30 last Tuesday evening after shunting operations, two men wearing trench coats accosted them. "Are you Daly?" asked one. "Are you Lynch?" queried the other. The drivers answered affirmatively. The accosters drew revolvers and fired point blank. Daly died; Lynch escaped with slight wounds. [15]

Harrington confirms, in his book Kerry Landing, that it was not the IRA who perpetrated this crime.[16] The subterfuge was the work of three officers from his own Free State Army Garrison.

"IN FACT DALY AND LYNCH WERE SHOT BY THREE FREE STATE OFFICERS. WITHOUT KNOWING THEIR INTENT, I SAW THEM LEAVE THE WORKHOUSE WHERE I WAS STATIONED, TO CARRY OUT THE CRIME. I ALSO SAW THEM RETURN. THEY WERE NOW IN UNIFORM AND THEY WORE TRENCH COATS." [17]

Torture methods adopted by certain officers during interrogation of IRA prisoners at Hartnett's Hotel in Castleisland the Free State Army HQ for the area, became known to the IRA. A native of Knocknagoshel named Lieutenant Patrick (Patie Pats) O'Connor, who was acting as an intelligence officer, became the prime target of the IRA for these alleged interrogation methods, and for being responsible for arrests in the Knocknagoshel area. Indeed, this Free State officer and his relationship with the Republican forces in his own area triggered much of the ferocity and the appalling direction which the Civil War took in Kerry.

It appears that a very personal grudge existed between O'Connor and the Republican forces in the Knocknagoshel area. It was the Republican interpretation of this grudge which led to the eventual killing of O'Connor. They believed that no

Republican from O'Connor's home parish of Knocknagoshel would survive the Civil War if O'Connor had been allowed to live. There is no doubt that O'Connor operated unusually extreme methods of interrogation in his singleminded pursuit of the IRA. Perhaps when one hears Republican accounts of the actions taken against the O'Connor family prior to Lieut O'Connor joining the Free State Army, one sees why he became so intent on wiping out the Knocknagoshel IRA.

Apparently, the local IRA became suspicious of Patie Pat's father, Patrick O'Connor in that they believed he was passing on names of local IRA men and locations of ambushes to the Free State authorities. One failed ambush which very nearly led to the total destruction of that column was at Jack Dautheen's Cross, on the Kilmanaghan road from Castleisland to Brosna. The normally punctual Free State patrol did not show and so after a two hour wait the IRA retreated. However, some time later the area was surrounded by a large force of Free State Army troops. O'Connor senior was seen conversing with Free State soldiers that morning.

However, to remove any doubt as to O'Connor's involvement with the Free State Army, the IRA decided to test the old man's loyalties by sending Patrick Buckley dressed as a Free State officer to interview him. O'Connor co-operated with what he thought was a Free State officer and even gave information about Buckley's own whereabouts, not recognising the IRA man.

The IRA decided to scare the family without loss of life as it was thought the old man may have divulged this information without any great animosity. The IRA believed he had to be punished or at least frightened sufficiently to prevent further passing of information to their enemies.

The local IRA forces took his cattle and pony trap. His belongings were removed from his property and distributed around the parish. However, unknown to the IRA they were observed and identified by O'Connor's son, Patie Pats who went on the following day to Castleisland and joined the Free

State Army. For the following six weeks he was to become the most deadly enemy and scourge of the Knocknagoshel IRA. Lieut. O'Connor knew everything about every IRA family in the intensely Republican Knocknagoshel area. When they killed him, his death was to trigger some of the worst atrocities in the whole Civil War.

Although some may disagree, in retrospect it seems to the author that the Knocknagoshel mine was the catalyst for the worst month in the history of the Civil War in Kerry. It was the beginning of what is now known as the Tragedies of Kerry. It all started as a result of the information passed on by old Patrick O'Connor, verified by Patrick Buckley and resulting in the confiscation of the O'Connor cattle by the IRA. The younger O'Connor would, as a result, become the terror of the local IRA. He was responsible for dozens of men sleeping in dugouts and in the ditches of the area as they were unable to return home because of O'Connor's nocturnal raids. A plan was devised by the IRA to strike at the heart of the Castleisland Garrison and to eliminate Lieut. O'Connor. It would lead five men to their deaths in Knocknagoshel.

Shortly after midnight on the night of March 5th, a large company of Free State Army officers and soldiers left Castleisland for Knocknagoshel, in the north-east of the county. By the time daylight dawned the five Free State troops, including Lt. O'Connor, two other Officers, and two soldiers were dead. One other soldier was appallingly wounded.

The author has visited the site of the Knocknagoshel mine where the three Free State officers and two soldiers lost their lives in the early hours of Tuesday, March 6th, 1923.

The scenic and peaceful, steeply inclined field, originally a wooded area called Baranarig Wood, at Meenbannivane near Knocknagoshel, in which the mine exploded, belies the terrible happenings of March 1923. The precise location of the explosion is exactly as it was 74 years ago, except that the wooded area surrounding the point of the explosion has been cleared of trees. Local people will say that bones of severed limbs and bits of shoe leather are mixed amongst the pile of exploded stone. A Sally tree grows out of the side of a mound on the steep, hilly field which runs down to the peacefully running little Tullaleague River at its southern boundary. The shattered stones from the slabs under which the mine exploded are still as they were when human remains of five men spilled over them on that March morning at 2 a.m. and set off a series of savage reprisals unparalleled in modern Irish history.

Former Kerryman Editor and lifelong Republican, Con Casey, [18] (interviewed in January 1996, when 97 years old), disputes the theory that Ballyseedy and the other Free State killings of March '23 were reprisals for Knocknagoshel as he believes the policy of mass killings of prisoners had come down from Free State HQ in Dublin shortly before the Knocknagoshel killings. Although Harrington stated that the sequence of reprisals commonly known afterwards as "The Tragedies of Kerry" was "deliberately planned by a clique of influential Dublin Guards officers in Ballymullen Barracks, Tralee and carried out in the vicinity of Tralee, Killarney and Cahirciveen." Harrington continued: "It is unknown how many Republican prisoners paid for the Knocknagoshel mine." Even after the IRA ceasefire of May 23rd, 1923, Volunteer Jerh. O'Leary was captured in Knocknagoshel and murdered in Hartnett's Hotel by Free State Army troops. [19]

The author's visit to Knocknagoshel in 1996 and 1997 was in the company of local farmer, Mícheál Walsh, who had an intimate knowledge and very personal family interest in these events.

Mícheál explained: "It was my uncle John (Coffey) Murphy, the local Blacksmith, who made the mines for the local IRA Unit. He made the Knocknagoshel mine too. Eventually he drank a lot before he died. He had made the mine that killed the five men and as a result his brother was murdered for it by the Free Staters. It wrecked our family through emigration and death." [20]

A number of Mícheál Walsh's family had been involved in

the total plot to assassinate Lieutenant O'Connor. Mícheál's aunt, local school teacher, Kathleen Walsh, wrote the note which Kathleen Hickey got delivered by a local schoolgirl. This communication containing fictitious details of a dugout at Baranarig Wood was to lead Officers O'Connor, Dunne and Stapleton, and enlisted soldiers O'Connor from Causeway, and Galvin from Killarney to their deaths.

The information in the note led the Free State Army and Lt. O'Connor to believe that there was a dugout in which ten or more IRA men, including leaders Humphrey Murphy and Mick McGlynn, were hiding. This was not the case as no such dugout existed in that field. Only a booby trap mine hidden under a large slab awaited the Free State troops. [21]

The mine had been brought to the so-called dugout on March 3rd by Johnny Nolan, Humphrey Murphy, Tom Heffernan, Mick McGlynn, John Murphy and Denis Walsh. Nolan had cycled 12 miles from Gleannthaune with the mine in a schoolbag strapped to the bar of his bicycle. It was primed on March 4th on the same day as Kathleen Walsh and Kathleen Hickey had sent the misleading message about the dugout intended for Officer Patie O'Connor. It was handed to a sentry at Castleisland Barracks. Lieut. O'Connor and up to 200 Free State troops surrounded the dugout during the early hours of March 5th and five of them were killed at approximately 2am when they were inspecting the "dugout".

Just almost three weeks later on March 24th, in the same field as the explosion, Free State soldiers Culhane, McAuliffe and Gaffney killed 23 year old Dan Murphy, who was a brother of John, the mine maker. They had arrested him at 5 a.m. and fired 21 bullets into his body at 11 a.m.. It was a case of mistaken identity as they thought they had the Blacksmith John who in fact, was the maker of the pipe mine. Kathleen Walsh and her three sisters, Joan, Bridie and Eileen were captured by the Free Staters and had their hair shaved under torture. They emigrated to the USA shortly afterwards. Though right handed, Kathleen had taken the precaution of writing the fatal note with her left hand. When interrogated after the explosion she reverted to her normal handwriting and was duly released. She emigrated shortly afterwards and died prematurely in 1940 in the USA.

Whether as a reprisal or not, the Ballyseedy atrocity followed within 24 hours of the March 5th Knocknagoshel mine killings. It was even more chilling in its calculated awfulness. It was followed by further atrocities as that week Kerry bled its way into the history books of Civil War horror.

Patrick Buckley was to lose his life in the Ballyseedy mine and only his tender age saved another Knocknagoshel youth, 17 year old Michael Walsh, who was a brother of Kathleen. It is recounted that the Free State officers changed their minds after first placing Walsh in the lorry for the fatal trip to Ballyseedy. Another Knocknagoshel man, Jer O'Leary, who was involved in the confiscation of the O'Connor cattle, eventually was shot in custody by the Free State troops at their Castleisland HQ after the Civil War was officially ended.

Dorothy Macardle's account of what is thought to be reprisals for the Knocknagoshel mine, while obviously partisan, is nonetheless worth recounting. Written in 1924, the Macardle work [22] is a record of the version of the events most likely believed by the Republicans of the time. She travelled to Kerry to interview witnesses and survivors of these times and while she sometimes erred on detail her description of these atrocities is the only source written at the time and still available today.

BALLYSEEDY MINE

Nine prisoners, John Daly, George O'Shea, Timothy Twomey, Patrick Hartnett, James O'Connell, John O'Connor, Patrick Buckley, James Walsh and Stephen Fuller, were being held for interrogation, along with many others, in Tralee Workhouse. According to Harrington, who was not a witness, on Wednesday, March 7th, they were brought to a point near Ballyseedy Cross, bound hand and foot and roped together in a circle, their backs to a log under which a mine had been placed. Eight of the nine were blown to bits.

The following account is taken from Macardle's 'Tragedies of Kerry'.

"THE PRISONERS WERE TAKEN IN SEPARATELY. WHEN SHANAHAN CAME OUT, HIS HEAD WAS COVERED WITH BLOOD AND HIS SPINE WAS INJURED, BUT HE WAS STILL ABLE TO WALK. THE PRISONERS WERE TAKEN OUT TO BE SHOT, AND SHOTS WERE FIRED ROUND THEIR HEADS. THEY WERE THEN SENTENCED, FOR THEIR OBDURATE SILENCE, TO BE EXECUTED AT MIDNIGHT AND WERE THEN LOCKED IN THEIR CELLS. AT MIDNIGHT STEPHEN FULLER HEARD HIS COMRADES BEING TAKEN OUT, ONE BY ONE, AND HEARD SHOTS FIRED IN THE YARD. THE GUARDS CAME FOR HIM AND TOOK HIM DOWN TO A DARK CELL. HE SAW NINE COFFINS THERE WITH THE LIDS CLOSED.

THREE OF THOSE HAVE THEIR MEN, THEY TOLD HIM, AND THIS IS YOURS, AND THEY STOOPED TO UNSCREW THE LID. FOR HALF AN HOUR MORE THEY WERE QUESTIONING HIM, HE WISHING ONLY FOR A SHARP END. THEN THEY LOCKED HIM INTO HIS CELL AGAIN.

THE PRISONERS WERE GIVEN SOME KIND OF TRIAL IN THE WORKHOUSE ON MARCH THE THIRD, BUT NO SENTENCE WAS TOLD. THEY WERE KEPT THERE FOR THREE DAYS MORE. SHANAHAN'S BACK HAD GROWN WEAK SINCE THE BEATING IN BALLYMULLEN, AND BEFORE MARCH THE SIXTH HE COLLAPSED. HIS ILLNESS SAVED HIM WHEN HIS COMRADES WERE TAKEN OUT.

IN THE EARLY HOURS OF WEDNESDAY (MARCH 7TH), JUST 24 HOURS AFTER KNOCKNAGOSHEL, WHILE IT WAS STILL DARK, STEPHEN FULLER WAS CALLED OUT OF HIS CELL. HE WAS TAKEN TO THE GUARDROOM. GEORGE O'SHEA AND TIMOTHY TWOMEY WERE WITH HIM AND THEY FOUND SIX MORE PRISONERS THERE.

THE PRISONERS LOOKED ILL; ONE HAD A BROKEN ARM; ALL WERE SCARRED AND BRUISED; JAMES WALSH HAD A BANDAGE ON HIS BROKEN WRIST. THE SOLDIERS SEARCHED THEM IN THE GUARDROOM AND TOOK THEIR CIGARETTES. THEY WERE PUT INTO A LORRY WITH A HEAVY ESCORT AND DRIVEN ALONG THE CASTLEISLAND ROAD. THEY WERE BEING TAKEN, THEY WERE TOLD, TO REMOVE BARRICADES. THEY DID NOT BELIEVE THAT - SICK MEN WITH USELESS HANDS AND ARMS.

ONE OF THE SOLDIERS HANDED EACH OF THEM A CIGARETTE. "THE LAST SMOKE YOU'LL HAVE," HE SAID.

THE LORRY PULLED UP NEAR THE CORNER OF THE KILLORGLIN ROAD, BESIDE BALLYSEEDY WOOD. THEY SAW A LOG LYING ACROSS THE ROAD. THEY

WERE MADE TO GET OUT OF THE LORRY AND STAND IN A CLOSE CIRCLE AROUND THE LOG.

THE SOLDIERS HAD STRONG ROPE AND ELECTRIC CORD. EACH PRISONER'S HANDS WERE TIED BEHIND HIM, THEN HIS ARMS WERE TIED ABOVE THE ELBOW TO THOSE OF THE MEN ON EITHER SIDE OF HIM. THEIR FEET WERE BOUND TOGETHER ABOVE THE ANKLES AND THEIR LEGS WERE BOUND TOGETHER ABOVE THE KNEES. THEN A STRONG ROPE WAS PASSED ROUND THE NINE AND THE SOLDIERS MOVED AWAY.

THE PRISONERS HAD THEIR BACKS TO THE LOG AND THE MINE, WHICH WAS BESIDE IT; THEY COULD SEE THE MOVEMENT OF THE SOLDIERS AND KNEW WHAT WOULD HAPPEN NEXT. THEY GRIPPED ONE ANOTHER'S HANDS, THOSE WHO COULD, AND PRAYED FOR GOD'S MERCY UPON THEIR SOULS.

THE SHOCK CAME, BLINDING, DEAFENING, OVERWHELMING. FOR STEPHEN FULLER IT WAS FOLLOWED BY A SILENCE IN WHICH HE KNEW THAT HE WAS ALIVE. THEN SOUNDS CAME TO HIM - CRIES AND LOW MOANS, THEN THE SOUNDS OF RIFLE FIRE AND EXPLODING BOMBS. THEN SILENCE AGAIN: THE WORK WAS DONE.

HE TURNED OVER; HE WAS NOT HURT; HE WAS LYING UNDER A DITCH IN THE WOOD. HIS CLOTHES WERE SCORCHED AND TORN TO SHREDS; CORDS WITH BURNT AND BROKEN ENDS WERE KNOTTED ON BOTH HIS WRISTS. THE EXPLOSION THAT KILLED THE TWO MEN TO WHOM HE WAS BOUND HAD SEVERED THE CORDS AND THROWN HIM, UNINJURED, INTO THE DITCH.

THE SOLDIERS HAD NO MEANS OF COUNTING THEIR VICTIMS. THEY WENT BACK TO THEIR BREAKFAST, AND STEPHEN FULLER CRAWLED AWAY TO SAFETY [23] TO A LOCAL IRA DUGOUT BEHIND MAY DALAIGH'S HOUSE AT CNOCAN, WHERE JOHN JOE SHEEHY AND HIS MEN HAD HEARD THE EXPLOSION. SHEEHY IMMEDIATELY PUBLICISED THE NEWS, CONTRADICTING FREE STATE CLAIMS THAT THE KILLINGS HAD BEEN THE RESULT OF AN ACCIDENT WHILE THE MINES WERE BEING TACKLED."

BACK IN TRALEE NINE COFFINS WERE PREPARED, BUT TO THE AMAZEMENT OF THE FREE STATE TROOPS, ONLY EIGHT BODIES WERE AVAILABLE TO FILL THEM.

THERE WAS MADNESS AMONG THE PEOPLE OF TRALEE. WHAT PRISONERS WERE IN THOSE COFFINS? NO ONE COULD TELL. THE COFFINS WERE OPENED IN THE STREETS BY MOTHERS, SISTERS AND WIVES, EACH PRAYING NOT TO FIND A FAMILIAR FACE.

The Free State Army official account of the Ballyseedy atrocity tried to explain away the carnage by saying that the Republican prisoners were being used by the army to clear barricades on the roadway from Tralee to Killarney. However, Stephen Fuller's son, Paudi, said his father's account of the terrible night never allowed for any doubt as to the intentions of the army command.

"My father was tied to the other eight prisoners in a circle around the mine. The blast burned the skin off his back. He was blown into the air and landed on his hands and knees. He was badly dazed but he realised that Patrick Buckley was also still alive. Buckley's injuries were horrific as he had almost been blown in two at the waist. He died in my father's arms and his last words were to say goodbye and advise my father to get out of danger and let people know what had happened."

"My father, then in a dazed state, was heading dangerously close to the army personnel when he realised the peril of the situation and turned towards the river. He waded through the water for a considerable distance where he found it very difficult to get a spot on the river bank to climb out of the river.

"According to my father that freezing March water cleansed his wounds and helped to save his life." [24]

The Free State Government issued a new regulation to their Kerry command:-

PRISONERS WHO DIE WHILE IN MILITARY CUSTODY IN THE KERRY COMMAND SHALL BE INTERRED BY THE TROOPS IN THE AREA IN WHICH THE DEATH HAS TAKEN PLACE. [25]

It was published in the Dublin press on the twenty-first of March 1923.

COUNTESS BRIDGE

On March 7, the day after the Ballyseedy atrocity just twenty miles away in Killarney another chapter in the tragedies of

Kerry was to be written. Niall Harrington described the incident when he said, shortly after Ballyseedy:

"FOUR REPUBLICAN PRISONERS WERE MURDERED IN THE SAME FOUL MANNER AT COUNTESS BRIDGE, KILLARNEY. FIVE HAD BEEN TAKEN OUT TO DIE AND AGAIN ONE ESCAPED - STEPHEN COFFEY OF BARLEYMOUNT. THE CRIMES WERE REPEATED ON MARCH 12TH, WHEN FIVE PRISONERS WERE TAKEN FROM THE WORKHOUSE NEAR CAHERCIVEEN. THERE WAS NO SURVIVOR." [26]

Harrington claims that the mines used in all three atrocities were constructed in Tralee by members of the Dublin Guards. He also believes that the evidence presented and the findings of the resulting military court of enquiry were "totally untrue". [27]

Marcadle's account of the tragedy continues:

"MEANWHILE, TWO YOUNG MEN, JEREMIAH DONOGHUE AND TADHG COFFEY, WERE CAPTURED IN COFFEY'S HOME, IN BARLEYMOUNT, ON THE 22ND OF FEBRUARY, 1923. COFFEY AND DONOGHUE WERE BROUGHT OUTSIDE AND PUT AGAINST A WALL AND THREATENED WITH INSTANT DEATH UNLESS THEY SAID WHERE THE REST OF THEIR COLUMN AND THE DUMP OF ARMS WERE TO BE FOUND. ON THEIR REFUSAL TO SPEAK, THEY WERE KICKED AND BEATEN.

THE PRISONERS WERE BROUGHT TO THE GREAT SOUTHERN HOTEL IN KILLARNEY, WHICH WAS BEING USED AS A BARRACKS. THE NIGHT THEY ARRIVED THERE, COFFEY WAS SUMMONED TO A ROOM WHERE FOUR OFFICERS WERE SITTING BY A FIRE. THEY STARTED INTERROGATING COFFEY AGAIN.

THE NEXT NIGHT COFFEY AND DONOGHUE WERE CHARGED, ON WILSON'S EVIDENCE, WITH BEING IN POSSESSION OF ARMS. THEY WERE SENTENCED TO EXECUTION AND PUT IN THE "CONDEMNED CELL". [28]

ON THE SATURDAY NIGHT THEY MET THREE MORE PRISONERS WHO HAD BEEN TAKEN THAT DAY IN A DUG-OUT. THEY WERE STEPHEN BUCKLEY OF RATHDRINAGH, DAN DONOGHUE OF LACCA AND TIM MURPHY OF RATHBREAN, AND THEY APPEARED TO HAVE BEEN BADLY BEATEN. [29]

THERE WAS AN ARMY TAILOR WHO WORKED IN THE BARRACKS CALLED SUGRUE, WHO WAS GREATLY TROUBLED ABOUT THE PRISONERS BUT DARED

NOT DO ANYTHING TO HELP THEM. ON OCCASION HE WOULD COME TO THE ROOM WHERE COFFEY AND DONOGHUE WERE AND LAY DOWN A BOTTLE OF STOUT, ASKING THE PRISONERS TO HIDE IT FOR GOD'S SAKE OR HE WOULD BE SHOT WITH THEMSELVES. ON THE SUNDAY HE TOLD THEM THAT THE NEWS WAS BAD AS HE HAD HEARD THEM PICKING A FIRING SQUAD THAT NIGHT. THE NEXT DAY, HOWEVER, HE CAME IN ALL SMILES TELLING THE PRISONERS THAT THEY WERE REPRIEVED.

THE PRISONERS KNEW WHAT THAT MEANT: THEY WERE HOSTAGES. WHEN THE NEXT REPUBLICAN MILITARY OPERATION TOOK PLACE THEY WOULD BE SHOT. [30]

THEIR FEARS WERE JUSTIFIED ON WEDNESDAY, THE SEVENTH OF MARCH, WHEN THEY WERE AWAKENED SUDDENLY. OUTSIDE, THE FIVE PRISONERS WERE MARCHED ALONG THE ROAD IN SINGLE FILE AND OVER THE FIELDS. WHEN THEY REACHED THE COUNTESS'S BRIDGE THEY WERE BROUGHT TO A HALT IN FRONT OF A LOW BARRICADE OF STONES WHICH RAN ACROSS THE ROAD. THEY WERE ORDERED TO MOVE THE STONES AND THROW THEM INSIDE THE FENCE.

THE PRISONERS RAN TO THE BARRICADE AND JUMPED OVER IT, THINKING THEY WERE TO BE SHOT WHILE MOVING THE STONES. THERE WAS A PAUSE AND THEN THEY SAW THE SOLDIERS RUNNING FOR COVER. THEN THE EXPLOSIONS CAME, BOMB AFTER BOMB WAS FLUNG AMONG THEM AND SHOTS WERE FIRED.

TADHG COFFEY AND JER DONOGHUE CRAWLED ON HAND AND KNEES AND GOT ROUND A BEND ON THE ROAD. MACHINE GUN FIRE WAS HITTING THE WALL BESIDE THEM. THEN DONOGHUE WAS HIT AND LAY STILL, DEAD. COFFEY KEPT GOING, CLIMBING A GATE INTO A WOOD AND RUNNING FOR ALL HE WAS WORTH. ALL THE TIME HE WAS THINKING IF HE COULD GET TO JACK MOYNIHAN'S HOUSE HE WOULD BE SAFE.

AHEAD IN THE DISTANCE HE SAW A HOUSE AND WONDERED IF HE WOULD TAKE THE CHANCE. NOT KNOWING WHERE MOYNIHAN'S WAS, HE FIGURED THE RISK WOULD HAVE TO BE TAKEN SOONER OR LATER."

AS IT HAPPENED THE RISK PROVED TO BE WELL WORTH TAKING BECAUSE BY SOME STRANGE COINCIDENCE THE HOUSE ACTUALLY TURNED OUT TO BE JACK MOYNIHAN'S. IN KILLARNEY TODAY, THE ENMITY OF THOSE TERRIBLE TIMES IS ETCHED IN STONE ON THE MONUMENT TO THE FOUR MEN KILLED AT COUNTESS BRIDGE.

The inscription reads: "In memory of Stephen Buckley, Jeremiah Donoghue, Daniel Donoghue, and Timothy Murphy. Soldiers of the IRA who were murdered here by Free State Forces on March 7, 1923."

CAHIRCIVEEN

FIVE DAYS LATER, IN CAHIRCIVEEN, ON MARCH 12TH, ANOTHER ATROCITY OCCURRED, WHICH COST THE LIVES OF FIVE MORE YOUNG MEN. THE FIVE MEN HAD BEEN CAPTURED AT A WAKE IN CORREVOOLA, A QUIET PLACE IN THE HILLS. THE PRISONERS, MIKE COURTNEY, JOHN SUGRUE, WILLIE RIORDAN, EUGENE DWYER AND DAN SHEA WERE TAKEN TO THE BAHAGHS WORKHOUSE, NEAR CAHIRCIVEEN.

ONE MORNING, SOME TIME AFTER THE MEN HAD BEEN ARRESTED, THE TOWN OF CAHIRCIVEEN WAS AWASH WITH RUMOURS. STRANGE OFFICERS HAD BEEN SEEN AT THE HOTEL. "IRREGULARS" HAD LAID A MINE - BUT HOW COULD THE IRREGULARS DO ANYTHING UP THERE NEAR THE FREE STATE BARRACKS? THAT ROAD WAS CONTROLLED NIGHT AND DAY BY THE SOLDIERS. SOMETHING HAD HAPPENED AT ANY RATE.

TWO NURSES, NURSE SLOAN AND NURSE O'CONNOR, WERE CALLED OUT. THEY MADE THEIR WAY UP THE ROAD TOWARDS BAHAGHS, WHERE THEY FOUND CLUMPS OF EARTH AND GRASS FLUNG EVERYWHERE AND GAPS IN THE ROAD; CARTRIDGE CASES WERE LYING ABOUT. THEY PICKED UP A CHAIN OF ROSARY BEADS - IT WAS SOAKED IN BLOOD. THEY CAME TO THE SHAMBLES THEN AND SAW WHAT (ACCORDING TO DOROTHY MACARDLE) IT WOULD NOT BE RIGHT TO DESCRIBE.

THAT NIGHT, THE TWELFTH OF MARCH, MESSAGES WERE SENT TO THE FAMILIES OF EACH OF THE FIVE MEN, TELLING THEM THAT THEIR SONS HAD BEEN KILLED AT DAYBREAK "IN A MINE EXPLOSION." NO MINE HAD BEEN LAID BY THE REPUBLICANS NEAR CAHIRCIVEEN.

THE OTHER PRISONERS IN BAHAGHS KNEW NOTHING UNTIL THE EVENING OF THE TWELFTH, WHEN A FREE STATE OFFICER, LIEUTENANT MCCARTHY, CAME IN TO THEM IN A VERY EXCITED STATE. HE CALLED A PRISONER NAMED JOHN GRAHAM, AND ASKED: "WHAT WAS SUPPOSED TO HAPPEN THE PRISONERS WHEN TAKEN OUT?" GRAHAM ANSWERED: "GOING TO BE REMOVED TO TRALEE." LIEUTENANT MCCARTHY THEN SAID:-

"THEY WERE MURDERED ON THE ROAD THIS MORNING BY THE MEN WHO
TOOK THEM OUT. I MYSELF AM PUTTING IN MY RESIGNATION THIS NIGHT. THE
FELLOWS THAT KILLED THEM WERE SOME OF THE DUBLIN GUARDS, WHO
WERE AT THE WORKHOUSE ON SUNDAY EVENING. ONE OF THEM WAS A
DIVISIONAL OFFICER. THE SERGEANT HAD NO ORDER TO GIVE THE KEY OF
THE ROOM TO ANYONE. MYSELF AND HEGARTY WENT TO BED. THE OTHER
FELLOWS WENT TO THE GUARDROOM AND TOLD THE SERGEANT TO COME
DOWN TO THE PRISONERS' ROOM, AND ONE OF THE GUARDS REFUSED TO GO.
HE THEN TOLD HIM HE WOULD BLOW HIS BRAINS OUT, AND BROUGHT HIM
DOWN AT THE POINT OF A REVOLVER. HE TOLD THE SERGEANT HE WAS TAK-
ING HIM AND HIS ESCORT, AND IF HE TOLD A WORD OF WHAT HAPPENED ON
THE WAY HE WOULD BLOW HIS BRAINS OUT. HE THEN TOOK THEM DOWN THE
ROAD. THERE WAS NO ATTEMPT TO ESCAPE, AS THE PRISONERS WERE SHOT
FIRST AND THEN PUT OVER A MINE AND BLOWN UP. IT WAS A FREE STATE
MINE, LAID BY THEMSELVES. I WILL GET THE STATEMENT PUT INTO THE PAPER.
THERE WERE SIX OR EIGHT IN THE LOT THAT MURDERED THEM. IT IS A MUR-
DER GANG THAT IS GOING AROUND TRYING TO KEEP THE WAR ON. WE OUR-
SELVES WILL SUPPORT THE FREE STATE GOVERNMENT AND FIGHT FOR IT, BUT
WE WILL NOT FIGHT FOR MURDER. WE WILL DO NO MORE WORK UNTIL THESE
FELLOWS ARE PROPERLY DEALT WITH." [31]

The following is an official statement from the O/C Kerry,
Third Brigade, and the O/C Operations, Kerry Brigade, with
reference to the so called mine and ambush mentioned in the
Portobello communique:

"THERE WAS NO AMBUSH IN THE VICINITY. ALL OUR TROOPS HAD BEEN
REMOVED FROM THE VICINITY OF CAHIRCIVEEN AND THE WORKHOUSE.
THERE WAS NO BARRICADE AND NO MINE LAID THERE BY US. THE FIVE PRIS-
ONERS HAD BEEN ARRESTED MORE THAN A WEEK PREVIOUSLY." [32]

In just one week, nineteen prisoners were put to death. The
five Free State Army men were blown to pieces at
Knocknagoshel and more tragedy was to follow, with a total of
twenty eight killings in Kerry before the 1st of April dawned.

CLASHMEALCON CAVES

THE STORY OF "AERO" LYONS AND HIS FIVE COMPANIONS AND HOW THEY STOOD SIEGE FOR THREE NIGHTS AND DAYS IN CLASHMEALCON CAVES.

IT WAS ON A DAY IN THE MIDDLE OF APRIL THAT FREE STATE TROOPS CAME TO CAUSEWAY TO MAKE A ROUND-UP. FROM DITCHES AND HOLLOWS ON EVERY SIDE, LYONS AND THE NINE MEN UNDER HIM KEPT THEM FIGHTING ALL DAY UNTIL AT NIGHTFALL THE OTHERS GAVE UP THE CHASE.

ONE OF LYONS' COMRADES, JIM MCENERY, WAS ARRESTED AFTER HIS HOUSE WAS RAIDED EARLY ON A SUNDAY MORNING. IF ONLY HE HAD BEEN TAKEN TO PRISON THEN... BUT HIS GUARDS LET HIM ESCAPE, AS THOUGH IT WAS MEANT; HE RAN OUT TO SEEK REFUGE AMONG THE CLIFFS.

LATER, MORE TROOPS CAME AND SURROUNDED THE HOUSE, NOT KNOWING WHAT HAD OCCURRED. HIS COMRADES SAW THEM FROM A HOUSE ACROSS THE ROAD AND TWO OF THEM, SHEA AND HATHAWAY, KNOWING NOTHING OF HIS ESCAPE, OPENED FIRE. JIM MCENERY, MEANWHILE, HAD BEEN SIGHTED AND WAS PURSUED. HIS FRIEND, TOM MCGRATH, SAW IT AND FIRED... HE RETREATED TO CLASHMEALCON AND THERE DISAPPEARED.

REINFORCEMENTS FROM THE FREE STATE POST AT BALLYHEIGUE, ADVANCING TO SURROUND MCENERY'S HOUSE, CAME UNDER THE CROSSFIRE FROM THEIR OWN TROOPS AND THE REPUBLICANS. THEY ALL SCATTERED OVER THE COUNTRY THEN.

THREE OF THE NINE HAD BEEN WARY AND GONE INLAND, BUT SIX MEN, LOSING, AS THOUGH BY SOME UNAVOIDABLE DOOM, ALL JUDGEMENT, WENT INTO DUMFORT'S CAVE.

THE FREE STATE TROOPS TOOK ONE PRISONER ON SUNDAY MORNING. HE WAS TOM MCGRATH'S BROTHER, JIM. THEY INTERROGATED HIM IN TRALEE BARRACKS BY THEIR INHUMAN METHODS UNTIL HE BROKE DOWN AND PROMISED TO TAKE THEM TO THE CAVES. IT WOULD DO LITTLE HARM, HE THOUGHT - THERE WAS NOBODY THERE.

VERY EARLY ON MONDAY MORNING HE CAME OUT WITH THE TROOPS TO CLASHMEALCON. THE SOLDIERS WATCHED FROM ABOVE WHILE HE CLAMBERED DOWN THE HALF-HIDDEN, PERILOUS PATH. HE WENT DOWN THE CLIFFS AND UP THE STEEP SLOPE OF SHINGLE TO THE MOUTH OF DUMFORT'S CAVE. AERO LYONS AND O'SHEA AND JIM MCENERY AND GREANEY...HATHAWAY, AND HIS OWN BROTHER, TOM WERE THERE. NOT ONE OF THEM BLAMED JIM MCGRATH. THEY TOOK HIM INTO THE CAVE. A SOLDIER TRIED TO FOLLOW

HIM BUT A BULLET FIRED FROM THE CAVE KILLED HIM INSTANTLY, AND HE FELL ON THE ROCKS BELOW. ONE MORE TRIED BUT WAS SHOT ALSO AND FELL INTO THE SEA. NO SOLDIER WOULD GO DOWN AFTER THAT.

EVENTUALLY, DARKNESS FELL AND THE SOLDIERS' EFFORTS SUBSIDED FOR THE NIGHT. ONE BY ONE THE MEN CREPT OUT FROM THE CAVE AND WALKED, BAREFOOT, OVER THE BOULDERS, TO THE RIGHT, ALONG BY THE FRIENDLY OVERSHADOWING ROCK WALL. THEY MOVED STEALTHILY, FOR FEAR OF STIRRING A PEBBLE, BETWEEN THE LONELY PINNACLE AND THE CLIFF, OUT OF THE CREEK AND ALONG TO THE FLAT ROCK OVER WHICH HUNG, THEY KNEW WELL, A LEDGE THEY WOULD BE ABLE TO CLIMB TO AND, ABOVE IT, ANOTHER CAVE. TOMMY MCGRATH AND PATRICK O'SHEA VOLUNTEERED TO GO FARTHER, TO TRY TO MAKE THEIR WAY OUT AND GET HELP...(THEY FAILED TO BREAK THROUGH AND DROWNED IN THE ATTEMPT).

WITH DAYLIGHT ON TUESDAY LORRY AFTER LORRY CAME FROM TRALEE WITH TROOPS AND MUNITIONS... A MACHINE GUN WAS PLACED ON THE POINT THAT COMMANDED THE CAVE. AN ARMOURED CAR WAS RUN OUT TO THE EDGE OF THE CLIFF. THE SOLDIERS WERE SWARMING ABOVE THE CLIFFS...

THE BOMBARDMENT OF THE CAVE WENT ON ALL DAY LONG WITH NO REPLY FROM THE SILENT CAVE. IT GAVE LYONS AND HIS MEN A BREATHER. THEY HAD SURVIVED ANOTHER DAY IN THE CAVES.

AERO LYONS HAD COME OUT ON TO THE LEDGE BELOW AND PUT UP HIS HANDS. THEY HAD BEEN STARVED OUT.

NOTES WERE PASSED UP AND DOWN BY CORDS. LYONS WAS TRYING TO MAKE TERMS. HE WOULD SURRENDER HIMSELF AND THE RIFLES ON CONDITION THAT THE REST SHOULD GO FREE. HIS ENEMIES WOULD HEAR OF NO SUCH TERMS.

IT WAS JUST MID-DAY WHEN A ROPE, BROUGHT OUT IN A LORRY, WAS LOWERED TO LYONS FROM THE CLIFFS, AND HE KNOTTED IT AND BEGAN TO CLIMB UP.

EXACTLY WHAT HAPPENED ON THE CLIFF'S EDGE IS NOT KNOWN. SOLDIERS BOASTED AFTERWARDS TO THEIR PRISONERS, THAT SOME OF THEM CUT THE ROPE; OTHER PEOPLE SAY THIS IS NOT TRUE; THE ROPE WAS THIN AND ROTTEN, IT IS SAID. ALL THAT IS KNOWN IS THIS: WHEN LYONS HAD ALMOST REACHED THE TOP, THE ROPE SNAPPED AND HE CRASHED ON THE ROCKS BELOW. LYONS LAY ON THE RIDGE OF THE ROCK BELOW, MAYBE A HUNDRED FEET DOWN. GREANEY, MCENERY AND HATHAWAY RAN TO HIM FROM THE

CAVE, BUT HE WAS RIDDLED BY GUN-FIRE WHERE HE LAY. WHEN THEY LIFTED HIM HE WAS DEAD.

ALL WAS QUIET FOR A WHILE. THEN THE REPUBLICANS STARTED SENDING UP MESSAGES TO THE FREE STATE OFFICERS' NOTES. A LITTLE WHILE LATER JIM MCENERY WAS BROUGHT UP. THEN GREANEY AND REGINALD HATHAWAY AND JIMMY MCGRATH WERE BROUGHT UP TO A NEARBY HOUSE, THEIR HANDS BOUND, THEY WERE THROWN ON THE FLOOR. SOME FEW HOURS LATER THEY WERE TAKEN OUT AND PUT INTO A LORRY AND DRIVEN OFF.

THE STORY OF THE FIGHT AT CLASHMEALCON CAVES WAS IN ALL THE PAPERS; FATHER TOM MCENERY, JIM'S BROTHER, HAD RUSHED HOME FROM ENGLAND; A PETITION FOR THE PRISONERS' LIVES WAS SIGNED BY THOUSANDS; RUMOURS WERE FLYING THROUGH TRALEE. THE PRISONERS, IT WAS SAID, HAD BEEN BEATEN ALMOST TO DEATH. FATHER TOM WAS ALL NIGHT AND DAY AT THE BARRACK GATE, BUT NO ONE WAS LET IN TO THEM AT ALL. HE TELEPHONED AGAIN AND AGAIN TO BRIGADIER O'DALY ASKING WHAT WAS TO BE DONE. HE GOT A DEFINITE ANSWER AT LAST.

"THEY'LL BE EXECUTED WHEN WE HAVE TIME." [33]

A report dated April 24th, 1923 from the Kerry Command at Ballymullen Barracks, Tralee to GHQ in Dublin outlined the ongoing day to day saga of the siege at Clashmealcon. It gives a graphic account of the action from the official Free State Army viewpoint. The more propagandised account of the action published in the Army Magazine, An t-Oglach of June 16th, 1923 is also of interest.

"OFFICE OF COMMAND REPORTS OFFICER

KERRY COMMAND
BALLYMULLEN BARRACKS
TRALEE
24TH APRIL 1923
TO:
G.S.O.
I/C. REPORTS,
PORTOBELLO BARRACKS,

DUBLIN.
TUESDAY 16TH APRIL;

TROOPS FROM TRALEE, CARRIED OUT EXTENSIVE SEARCHES IN CAUSEWAY AREA, THIS MORNING. IN COURSE OPERATIONS A PLACE CALLED CLASH, ONE OF THE MOST REMOTE POINTS ON KERRY COAST WAS INVESTED. FIVE MEN INCLUDING AN OFFICER DESCENDED THE CLIFFS TO THE BEACH, ABOUT ONE HUNDRED FEET BELOW - AND WERE ABOUT TO ENTER THE CAVE - WHEN THEY ENCOUNTERED A STONE BARRICADE. THEY REMOVED IT - ONLY TO FIND A SECOND ONE A FEW YARDS INSIDE THE MOUTH OF THE CAVE. AS THEY WERE PROCEEDING TO REMOVE THE SECOND BARRICADE HEAVY RIFLE FIRE WAS OPENED FROM INSIDE THE CAVE.

VOLUNTEER O'NEILL, A NATIVE OF DUBLIN WAS KILLED OUTRIGHT AND LIEUT. PEARSON, OF THE ENGINEERS - SERIOUSLY WOUNDED. THE REMAINING MEN ENDEAVOURED TO ASCEND THE STEEP PATH TO THE TOP OF THE CLIFF - BUT WERE BEATEN BACK BY FIRE FROM THE CAVE ENTRANCE WHICH DIRECTLY FACED THE PATH.

FINALLY, ROPES HAD TO BE LOWERED OVER THE EDGE AND IN THIS WAY LIEUT. PEARSON, AND THE TWO OTHER MEN WERE BROUGHT TO SAFETY. EVERY ATTEMPT TO RECOVER BODY OF DEAD VOLUNTEER WAS MET WITH HEAVY FIRE FROM IRREGULARS, AND THE BODY STILL LIES ON THE BEACH. REINFORCEMENTS FROM TRALEE, LATER TRIED TO SMOKE OCCUPANTS OUT OF THE CAVE AND LOWERED BURNING SACKS OF HAY AND TURF - OVER CLIFF'S EDGE TO CAVE ENTRANCE. THIS HAD NOT DESIRED EFFECT - AND MINES WERE THEN LOWERED AND EXPLODED WITH WHAT EFFECT IS NOT YET KNOWN. AT PRESENT MOMENT THE IRREGULARS WHO NUMBER EIGHT HAVE NOT LEFT THE CAVE, TO WHICH THE TROOPS ARE LAYING SIEGE. IRREGULARS HAVE NO HOPE OF ESCAPE AS THERE IS ONLY ONE EXIT.

WEDNESDAY, 17TH APRIL

SIEGE OF CAVE AT CLASH STILL CONTINUES. TRAPPED IRREGULARS SHOWING NO SIGNS OF SURRENDER. MORE MINES LOWERED OVER CLIFF AND EXPLODED TODAY. EFFECT ON OCCUPANTS OF CAVE UNKNOWN.

LOCAL PEOPLE STATE THERE IS NO MEANS OF ESCAPE. BODY OF VOLUNTEER O'NEILL, HOME ADDRESS - 14 GRANVILLE STREET, DUBLIN, RECOVERED BY RED CROSS TODAY. HAD TO BE DRAWN UP BY ROPES.

THURSDAY, 18TH APRIL

LIEUT. PIERSON, WOUNDED IN CAVE FIGHT SUCCUMBED THIS MORNING. THE SITUATION AT CLASH STILL REMAINS UNCHANGED.

FRIDAY, 19TH APRIL

THE CAVE SIEGE AT CLASH, ENDED LAST EVENING. THE PREVIOUS NIGHT THE IRREGULARS, UNDER COVER OF DARKNESS MADE A DASH TO ANOTHER CAVE. TWO OF THEM WERE DROWNED IN THE ATTEMPT - THOMAS MCGRATH AND PATRICK O'SHEA.

THE REMAINING FIVE REACHED THEIR OBJECTIVE. HEAVY FIRE WAS MAINTAINED BY TROOPS ALL DAY YESTERDAY, FROM CLIFF. THE LEADER OF THE IRREGULARS - KNOWN AS "AEROPLANE" LYONS, O/C. 2ND BATTALION, KERRY NO. I. BRIGADE, WAS KILLED - AND WASHED OUT TO SEA.

THE SURVIVORS THEN SURRENDERED AND WERE HAULED UP BY ROPES. THE PRISONERS INCLUDE - JAMES MCINERNY, REGINALD HATHAWAY AND EDWARD GREANY. THEY WERE IN A EXHAUSTED STATE AND HAD BEEN DRINKING SEA-WATER FOR A WHOLE DAY. MCINERNY & GREANY, WERE IN CUSTODY AT THE TIME PIERCE SURRENDERED AND BEING MEMBERS OF HIS COLUMN, WERE RELEASED FOR THE FURTHER PROMOTION OF PEACE - ON SIGNING THE FORM.

GREANY HAD BEEN ARRESTED WITH A RIFLE AND AMMUNITION. HATHAWAY - ALIAS - WALTER STEPHENS, IS A ENGLISH MAN A NATIVE OF LONDON - WHO DESERTED MONTHS AGO. HE JOINED THE NATIONAL ARMY - AND DESERTED WITH A RIFLE AND A HUNDRED ROUNDS OF AMMUNITION. WHEN PREVIOUSLY ARRESTED HE GAVE A FICTITIOUS - WALTER STEPHENS, AND WAS IN POSSESSION OF FIRE ARMS. HE ALSO WAS RELEASED ON SIGNING FORM AT TIME OF PIERCE'S SURRENDER. IN THE CLASH SIEGE THE TROOPS CAPTURED TWO RIFLES AND ONE COLT REVOLVER. THREE RIFLES WERE SWEPT AWAY WITH THE TIDE. IN THE SUBSEQUENT SEARCH OF THE CAVE CIVIC GUARD UNIFORMS WERE DISCOVERED WITH QUANTITY OF BEDDING. THESE WERE TAKEN WHEN LYONS AND HIS COLUMN RECENTLY BURNED CIVIC GUARD STATION AT BALLYHEIGUE AND STRIPPED OCCUPANTS.

TWO IRREGULARS NAMED HARRINGTON, AND DALTON WERE CAPTURED WITH TWO RIFLES IN BALLYDUFF DISTRICT NORTH KERRY THIS MORNING.

SATURDAY, 20TH APRIL

FIVE IRREGULARS SURRENDERED IN KENMARE, SIX OTHERS CAPTURED. TROOPS OPERATING IN SCARTAGLIN DISTRICT, CASTLEISLAND, AMBUSHED AT BARNA. ONE IRREGULAR KILLED ONE PRISONER CAPTURED.[34]

*The above report was sent by the Kerry Command, Tralee, at the time the siege at Clashmealcon had just ended but an interesting report, written and published on the Internal Army Magazine of June 16th, 1923, gives an official eyewitness account from the Free State Army point of view. The report in An t-Oglach goes as follows:

THE CAVES OF CLASHMEALCON
Eye-witness's Dramatic Story of Heroic Deeds on the Wild Kerry Coast.

"One of the most heroic and strikingly dramatic incidents in the history of the army, occurred in April last, when an officer and a Volunteer lost their lives as the result of an encounter with a party of Irregulars, secreted in a cave at a spot called Clashmealcon in North Kerry.

A sergeant and a Volunteer were the only survivors among the four men who attempted to enter the cave. Their rescue and that of the wounded officer (who died subsequently), the recovery of the body of the dead Volunteer, and the events preceding the surrender of the Irregulars three days later, are set forth in the following graphic narrative from an eye witness which contains a wealth of details not hitherto published."

"At midnight on Sunday, April 14th, a small party of men left Ballymullen Barracks, Tralee, to carry out a search of the Ballyduff district in North Kerry, where it was believed that a column of Irregulars, known as "Aeroplane Lyons Column" was in hiding.

Ballyduff and Causeway districts were invested and searched without result and at 9 o'clock on Monday morning the troops found themselves standing on the precipitous cliffs at Clashmealcon, one of the wildest and bleakest spots on the Shannon shore. 120 feet below them lay the beach.

It was decided to carry out a search of caves on the beach. The hazardous descent was made by four men - Lieut. H.A. Pierson, attached to the Engineers, McCluskey, Volunteer James O'Neill

AND VOLUNTEER MCCARTHY. THEY CRAWLED DOWN THE STEEP PATH AND, ON REACHING THE BEACH, FOUND THEMSELVES IN FRONT OF A CAVE. AT ITS MOUTH THEY ENCOUNTERED A STONE BARRICADE. THIS, THEY REMOVED, ONLY TO FIND A FEW YARDS FURTHER ON A SECOND ONE. AS THEY WERE PRO-CEEDING TO KNOCK DOWN THE STONES, HEAVY RIFLE FIRE WAS OPENED ON THEM FROM THE INTERIOR.

IN THE FIRST VOLLEY, VOLUNTEER O'NEILL WAS KILLED OUTRIGHT AND LIEUT. PIERSON WOUNDED. THE REMAINING TWO MEN WERE FORCED TO RETIRE SOME THIRTY YARDS FOR COVER - AS NO COVER EXISTED AT THE CAVE MOUTH.

FIRE WAS KEPT UP AS THEY CREPT ALONG THE SHORE TO THE SAFETY AFFORDED BY A ROCK. WHEN THE FIRING DIED AWAY, THEY ATTEMPTED TO RESCUE LIEUT. PIERSON, BUT EVERY ATTEMPT WAS MET WITH RENEWED FIRE FROM THE OCCUPANTS OF THE CAVE.

RED CROSS MEN THEN ENDEAVOURED TO RESCUE THE WOUNDED OFFICER, BUT EVERY TIME THEY SHOWED THEMSELVES A VOLLEY OF RIFLE FIRE CRASHED FROM THE CAVE.

AND SO FOR FOUR LONG HOURS THE OFFICER LAY BLEEDING ON THE SANDS TILL AT LAST ONE DESPERATE EFFORT BY THE MEN TRAPPED ON THE BEACH BROUGHT HIM TO THE COMPARATIVE SAFETY OF THE ROCK.

IT WAS NOW THAT A GREATER DIFFICULTY AROSE - HOW TO BRING HIM TO THE CREST OF THE CLIFF. THE PATH BY WHICH THEY HAD DESCENDED WAS COMMANDED BY THE OCCUPANTS OF THE CAVE. TO ATTEMPT TO ASCEND IT WOULD BE NOTHING BUT SUICIDE. THE ONLY COURSE OPEN WAS TO LOWER ROPES OVER THE CLIFF'S EDGE AND HAUL UP THE WOUNDED OFFICER AND THE TWO SURVIVORS.

IT WAS A PERILOUS ASCENT MADE UNDER ENEMY FIRE, FOR THE MOMENT THE FORM OF THE OFFICER APPEARED SWINGING IN THE OPEN, A FURTHER VOLLEY OF FIRE CAME FROM THE CAVE. HE WAS DRAGGED TO SAFETY, HOW-EVER; AND THE RESCUE OF SERGEANT MCCLUSKEY AND VOLUNTEER MCCARTHY WAS THEN SUCCESSFULLY NEGOTIATED. THEY ALSO HAD TO RUN THE GAUNTLET OF THE ENEMY'S FIRE.

THE BODY OF VOLUNTEER O'NEILL LAY ON THE SANDS, FACE DOWN-WARDS, WITH ARMS AND LEGS OUTSTRETCHED. THE MORNING WAS BRIGHT

AND CLEAR AND SHAFTS OF SUNLIGHT PLAYED ON THE GREEN-CLAD FORM. A RED PATCH OF BLOOD SHOWED ON THE SANDS NEARBY.

TO THE LEFT WAS A MOSS COVERED ROCK, CRIMSON DASHED STAINED. ON THIS ROCK LIEUT. PIERSON, HAD REMAINED FOR HOURS, STRIVING TO STAUNCH THE FLOW OF BLOOD FROM HIS LEGS UNTIL HE WAS FINALLY RESCUED.

ALL AROUND ONE SAW NOTHING BUT BEETLING CLIFFS AND THE SEA THUNDERED AGAINST THE ROCKS. IT WAS A GRIM, FORBIDDING SPOT, FIT SETTING FOR THE TRAGEDY THAT HAD TAKEN PLACE.

STANDING ON THE CLIFF'S EDGE, COMRADES OF THE DEAD VOLUNTEER GAZED DOWN ON THE BODY WHICH WAS ALREADY BEING ENCIRCLED BY THE FAST-APPROACHING TIDE. "POOR GINGER" ONE OF THEM MUTTERED. "HE INSISTED ON COMING OUT WITH US, ALTHOUGH HE WAS NOT SUPPOSED TO GO OUT ON STUNTS." (VOLUNTEER O'NEILL WAS EMPLOYED AS AN ORDERLY AT COMMAND HEADQUARTERS, TRALEE.

THE TIDE CAME SWEEPING IN AND SOON THE BODY WAS BEING TOSSED ABOUT AMONG THE ROCKS - THE HELPLESS PLAYTHING OF THE WAVES.

THE MEN ON THE CLIFF WERE POWERLESS TO EFFECT ANYTHING, FOR SEVERAL EFFORTS ON THE PART OF RED CROSS MEN TO CLIMB DOWN ON THE BEACH RESULTED IN FIRE BEING OPENED FROM THE CAVE.

AND SO THE BODY REMAINED ON THE BEACH BUFFETED BACKWARDS AND FORWARDS UNTIL AT LAST THE TIDE RECEDED AND LEFT IT LYING ON A JUTTING ROCK STARING WITH UNSEEING EYES AT THE HEAVENS.

BY THIS TIME, REINFORCEMENTS HAD ARRIVED FROM TRALEE. IT WAS SEEN FROM THE BEGINNING THAT THE ONLY WAY TO BRING ABOUT A SURRENDER WAS BY EITHER STARVING THE IRREGULARS INTO SUBMISSION, OR SMOKING THEM OUT OF THEIR FORTRESS (IF THAT COULD POSSIBLY BE ACHIEVED).

LARGE QUANTITIES OF HAY AND TURF WERE PROCURED AND PLACED IN SACKS WHICH WAS SATURATED WITH PARAFFIN AND PETROL. THESE WERE SET ALIGHT AND LOWERED OVER THE CLIFF TO THE CAVE MOUTH. BEFORE THE LONG DENSE CLOUDS OF SMOKE COMPLETELY OBSCURED OUT THE VIEW OF THE CAVE, AND FOR SEVERAL HOURS THE BLAZE CONTINUED.

THE HEAVY PALL LIFTED ABOUT 4 O'CLOCK AND WE COULD SEE THE SMOKE WREATHING IN SPIRALS INTO THE CAVE. BUT THERE WAS NO SIGN OF SURRENDER FROM WITHIN.

IT WAS THEN DECIDED TO SEE WHAT EFFECT A MINE WOULD HAVE ON THE SITUATION. ONE WAS LOWERED OVER THE CLIFF AND EXPLODED.

A TREMENDOUS REVERBERATION AWOKE THE WHOLE COUNTRYSIDE, AND THOUSANDS OF PIECES OF ROCK WERE SENT HURTLING THROUGH THE AIR.

NO SIGN OF LIFE FROM THE CAVE. A SECOND MINE WAS EXPLODED WITH THE SAME RESULT. A BATTERY OF MACHINE GUNS THEN TRIED OPERATIONS ON THE CAVE MOUTH BUT WITHOUT APPARENT EFFECT. SPASMODIC FIRING HAD COME FROM THE CAVE BEFORE THE MINE EXPLOSIONS, BUT NONE SINCE. "THEY MUST BE DEAD, THE CONCUSSION KILLED THEM." THIS THEORY WENT THE ROUNDS, BUT ONE FELT IT WAS TOO RISKY TO ACCEPT IT AS TRUE AND MAKE THE DESCENT TO THE BEACH.

SO THROUGHOUT THE NIGHT THE SIEGE WAS MAINTAINED. TROOPS KEPT VIGIL ALL AROUND THE CLIFF'S EDGE. LAMPS WERE LOWERED OVER THE CLIFF WHEN DARKNESS SET IN BUT THEY AFFORDED VERY FEEBLE LIGHT; AND, AS WAS AFTERWARDS LEARNED, THE IRREGULARS MADE A DASH, UNOBSERVED, DURING THE NIGHT TO ANOTHER CAVE. TWO OF THEM WERE DROWNED IN THE ATTEMPT.

ALL DAY ON TUESDAY THE SIEGE CONTINUED. THE TROOPS EXPLODED THREE MINES ON THE BEACH BUT THERE WAS NO RESPONSE FROM THE IRREGULARS. THE MACHINE GUNNERS THEN SWEPT THE MOUTH OF THE CAVE WITH A BARRAGE. NO SIGN FROM THE TRAPPED ENEMY. DURING THE DAY A PRIEST ARRIVED ON THE SCENE AND REQUESTED THAT THE IRREGULARS BE GIVEN A CHANCE OF MAKING THEIR PEACE WITH GOD. HE WAS INFORMED THAT EVERY FACILITY WOULD BE GIVEN HIM TO GO DOWN TO THE CAVE, AND THAT OUR FIRE WOULD BE WITHHELD DURING THE TIME HE WAS DESCENDING THE CLIFF, HEARING CONFESSIONS IN THE CAVE, AND COMING BACK TO TERRA FIRMA. THIS DID NOT SATISFY THE PRIEST. HE REQUIRED A GUARANTEE FROM THE TROOPS THAT THE IRREGULARS WOULD NOT FIRE ON HIM. THE IMPOSSIBLE NATURE OF THIS REQUEST WAS POINTED OUT TO HIM, WHEREUPON HE INTIMATED HE WOULD GO DOWN TO THE CAVE IF SOME OF THE TROOPS ACCOMPANIED HIM. NONE OF US FELT DISPOSED TO AGREE TO THIS AND A LITTLE LATER THE CLERGYMAN DEPARTED.

THE BODY OF VOLUNTEER O'NEILL WAS STILL LYING ON THE BEACH, AND, ON NOON ON TUESDAY, TWO MEDICAL ORDERLIES - VOLUNTEERS BROPHY AND MULREADY, PLUCKILY OFFERED TO GO DOWN AND FETCH IT UP. A ROPE WAS FLUNG DOWN TO THE BEACH AND THE BODY OF THE DEAD VOLUNTEER WAS BROUGHT UP. THE TWO ORDERLIES DIRECTED THE COURSE

OF THE BODY, THUS PREVENTING IT FROM STRIKING AGAINST THE ROCKS ON THE WAY UP. THEY FINALLY CLAMBERED UP, BREATHLESS AFTER THEIR EXERTIONS.

TUESDAY NIGHT ON THE SAME VIGIL, DAWN BROKE. NO SIGN OF LIFE ON THE BEACH OR IN THE CAVES. A TURBULENT DASHED ANGRILY AGAINST THE ROCKS, SPRAYING THE CAVES WITH FOAM. THERE SEEMED LITTLE HOPE FROM ESCAPE FROM DROWNING FOR THE IRREGULARS. WHILE WE WERE WONDERING WHAT WOULD HAPPEN NEXT A SHRILL WHISTLE SOUNDED FROM BELOW. THE FIGURE OF A MAN STOOD AT THE MOUTH OF A CAVE, GESTICULATING WILDLY. BY SIGNS HE MADE IT KNOWN TO US THAT HE WANTED A ROPE LOWERED. THIS WAS DONE AND TO THE ROPE HE ATTACHED A NOTE OFFERING TO SURRENDER AND TELLING OF THE DEATHS OF DROWNING OF TWO OF HIS MEN. IT WAS SIGNED "AEROPLANE LYONS".

A NOTE WAS SENT BACK BY THE SAME MEANS, ASKING THAT ALL GUNS BE TIED TO THE ROPE. THREE RIFLES WERE THUS SURRENDERED. THE REMAINING THREE HAD BEEN WASHED AWAY BY THE TIDE ON THE NIGHT THE IRREGULARS HAD MADE THE FATAL DASH FROM ONE CAVE TO ANOTHER. THE IRREGULAR LEADER WAS ENDEAVOURING TO GET AWAY FROM THE CAVE WHEN HE CAME UNDER FIRE AND WAS MORTALLY WOUNDED. THE OTHER OCCUPANTS DID NOT SHOW THEMSELVES FOR SOME HOURS AFTERWARDS. BY THEN, THE BODY OF "AEROPLANE LYONS" HAD BEEN WASHED OUT TO SEA AND WATER WAS POURING INTO THE CAVE.

IT WAS LATE IN THE AFTERNOON WHEN THE FOUR REMAINING IRREGULARS APPEARED ON THE BEACH AND SIGNIFIED SURRENDER. THEY WERE HAULED UP THE CLIFF AND PRESENTED A DISHEVELLED AND HAGGARD APPEARANCE. THREE OF THEM HAD PREVIOUSLY BEEN RELEASED ON SIGNING THE FORM OF UNDERTAKING, AND, ONE OF THEM WAS AN ENGLISHMAN AND A DESERTER FROM THE BRITISH ARMY."[35]

*This dramatic official account, published by the Free State Army in their Magazine, would, just as in Dorothy Macardle's account of the same tragedy, need to be understood as a biased account.

The prisoners captured at Clashmealcon were executed at dawn on April the 25th, on the day after the latter report was sent to GHQ in Dublin.

"IT WAS ON THE EIGHTEENTH THAT AERO LYONS WAS KILLED. ON THE FIFTH OF MAY HIS BODY CAME UP FROM THE SEA. PATRICK O'SHEA'S AND TOM MCGRATH'S BODIES THE SEA HOLDS STILL." [36]

The Clashmealcon Caves siege, on the Shannon side of Kerry Head was the last major episode of the war in Kerry. Harrington in his more balanced account confirms that Lyons was "riddled" with bullets having fallen to the rocks below and that two Free State soldiers were shot dead from the caves. The other men who surrendered were sentenced to death and were executed in Ballymullen Barracks, Tralee, on April 25, 1923. [37]

In the middle of the tiny village of Kilflynn, the graveyard holds two graves with great significance from the Civil War in Kerry. A large Celtic cross dominates the centre of the graveyard overlooking the road. In it Aero Lyons, the leader of the Kilflynn men killed in the action at Clashmealcon, is remembered. Just a few yards away a black marble headstone marks the spot where his Kilflynn neighbour and IRA comrade, Stephen Fuller, the sole survivor of Ballyseedy is buried. He lived sixty one years after the tragedies of Kerry of that infamous spring of 1923.

Reginald Hathaway was executed by firing squad at Ballymullen Barracks after defecting to the IRA. Eighty seven year old Jack Kirby of Lisodigue remembers the day his father directed the young soldier, Hathaway, who was in full battle kit to join up with an IRA column in Currahane, between the villages of Fenit and Ardfert. [38] Hathaway had deserted his British Army regiment in Tralee to join the IRA during the War of Independence. He took the Anti-Treaty side during the Civil War and paid for the decision with his life. [39]

The Civil War in Kerry was a cruel and unforgiving time in our history. Such merciless acts perpetrated by both sides burned deep in the memory and heart of that generation and indeed generations to come.

Again I would like to reiterate my reasons for including this gruesome chapter in the book. I believe it was necessary so as to highlight the darkest days of 1923. It demonstrates how that generation was able to put that horrific experience to one side after the Civil War, with the help of the uniting force of the GAA and Gaelic football. Now in the profiles to follow you will see that the resultant hatred of the Civil War was overcome because of, and for the sake of, Gaelic football in Kerry.

Chapter Notes

(1) Hopkinson, Michael. Green Against Green, p240

(2) Hopkinson, Michael. Green Against Green, p273.

(3) TV Documentary. Dollard interview on WW2.

(4) Quilter, Sean. Statement. August 1997.

(5) Freeman's Journal. Notice signed by Paddy O'Daly re shortages, etc.

(6) Keating, Dan. Interview 1997.

(7) Barrett, Kitty. Interview.

(8) Harrington, Niall C. Kerry Landing. p141.

(9) W.R.E. Murphy. Letter to Commander in Chief. Dublin Oct. 1st. 1922.

(10) Hopkinson, Michael. Green Against Green. p240

(11) Hopkinson, Michael. Green Against Green. p240.

(12) Harrington, Niall C. Kerry Landing. p141 and p143.

(13) Hopkinson, Michael. Green Against Green. p240.

(14) Freeman's Journal January 27th 1923 in Harrington's Kerry Landing. p147.

(15) Harrington, Niall C. Kerry Landing p147.

(16) Ibid.

(17) Ibid.

(18) Casey, Con. Interview. 1996.

(19) Harrington, Niall C. Kerry Landing. p149.

(20 Walsh, Mícheál. Interview. 1997.

(21) Ibid.

(22) Macardle, Dorothy. Tragedies Of Kerry.

(23) Macardle, Dorothy. Tragedies Of Kerry. "Ballyseedy", p19. Ed 1990.

(24) Fuller, Paudie. Interview 1997.

(25) Macardle, Dorothy. Tragedies Of Kerry. "Ballyseedy . p19 Ed 1990.

(26) Harrington, Niall C. Kerry Landing. p149.

(27) Ibid.

(28) Macardle, Dorothy. Tragedies Of Kerry. Ed 1991. p21.

(29) Ibid p22.

(30) Macardle, Dorothy. Tragedies Of Kerry. Ed 1991 p23.

(31) Visit to Monument 1997. See Pic page

(32) Macardle, Dorothy. Ed 1991 p43.

(33) Ibid p43.

(34) Official Report Kerry Command on Clashmealcon 24-4-23.

(35) Official Report..... An tOglach 16-6-23.

(36) Macardle, Dorothy. Ed 1991. Tragedies Of Kerry, Clashmealcon Caves p54 to p63.

(37) Harrington, Niall C. Kerry Landing. p151.

(38) Kirby, Jack. Interview 1997.

(39) Harrington, Niall C. Kerry Landing. p37.

Chapter 5
The Bridge builders

John Joe Sheehy was the most senior member of the six Kerry footballers I will profile in the following pages. Con Brosnan was three years younger, born in 1900. They were the two leading protagonists in the examples of devotion to game and country. They may have met through football before the War of Independence began but they were living 25 miles apart, which in those days was a considerable distance. However, as they were both in the GAA and in the Volunteers one could almost certainly assume that they were aware of each other's presence.

During the War of Independence and the lack of football activity, their prowess as footballers was halted but, correspondingly, their IRA activity took over their lives. Next in line in their age group came Joe Barrett who was born in 1902. Coming from the same town, Barrett and Sheehy would have known each other. Their membership of the Volunteers would have made them aware of each other too, although the age gap at that stage would have limited their contact. Sheehy would have known Joe's older brother, Christy, better, through the early Volunteer years and the limited Tralee Street League.

Barrett and Brosnan would not have known each other well until they shared the Kerry jersey in 1923, although Barrett would have been aware of Brosnan's reputation as a freedom fighter in the War of Independence.

By the time young Purty Landers came on the political scene as a Fianna Boy in the early '20s, Joe Barrett, five years older, would have known his family as neighbours and friends. Purty's older brother, Bill, was a fellow member of No 1 Battalion, Kerry Number I Brigade IRA, (the Rock Street Area) with Barrett.

Our other two football personalities profiled in this book,

Tim O'Donnell and the youngest of the six, Johnny Walsh, through age and geographical circumstances, would not have met the other four players profiled until their football paths crossed towards the end of the 1920s. O'Donnell was born in 1907 and lived on the Dingle Peninsula and Johnny Walsh was born in 1911 in Ballylongford, North Kerry.

At the heart of the War of Independence, in 1920, Purty Landers was thirteen, Joe Barrett was eighteen, Con Brosnan was twenty, and John Joe Sheehy was twenty three. To the reader of the 1990s these ages must seem exceedingly youthful indeed to carry such responsibility. Some of the most active members in the guerilla warfare in the Anglo-Irish War ranged from mid teens to early thirties.

It was a young man's fight. Kevin Barry was eighteen years old when he was hanged in Mountjoy Jail, in November 1920. Cork hurler Jim Hurley, another Cork Battalion leader and "certainly one of the best in Ireland," according to Commandant General Tom Barry, leader of the most devastating Flying Column during the War of Independence, was only eighteen. Barry himself was only twenty two. Dan Breen was twenty six when he was one of the most hunted men in Ireland. When Michael Collins was shot in August 1922, having broken the British Empire, he was a mere thirty two years of age, and twenty six in the GPO in 1916.

When the football powers of these six players gradually emerged from the turbulent political years of the War of Independence and the Civil War it was to bear such fruit and set a foundation stone so that in the following two decades from 1923 to '41 Kerry would win eleven all Ireland titles. Statisticians would come up with various computations but, roughly speaking, Kerry won an All Ireland in less than every eighteen months, taking into account that they stood down twice in that time. Kerry won the 1924 All Ireland Final in 1925, and in the 15 years in which they competed from 1925 to 1941, Kerry won eleven All Ireland titles. The seed of this harvest was set by the Kerry team which emerged from the Civil War and blazed a trail through the '20s into the early '30s, culminating in the four-in-a-row of All Ireland titles from 1929 to 1932. Two of our personalities, John Joe Sheehy and Con Brosnan, captained one each, and Joe Barrett captained two of those titles, giving his third captaincy to his friend and one time political foe, Con Brosnan.

Chapter 6

John Joe Sheehy

Born in 1897, John Joe Sheehy was the oldest member of the group of six Kerry players into whose interesting lives we are about to dip. I will endeavour to illustrate the backgrounds which produced their differing political outlooks. One will wonder how, coming from so many varying upbringings, they each ended up with one major interest in common, their love for Gaelic football. He completed his football career with four All Ireland medals to his credit. He also played for Kerry and Munster.

It is curious to see how each of the personalities in the book overcame the dilemma of playing Gaelic football with their county in the era of such turbulent political upheaval, distrust and widespread hatred evident in their county. John Joe Sheehy is one of the greatest examples.

Sheehy was an unwavering Republican all of his adult life. However, his son Brian could not detect any strong Nationalist outlook in his father's upbringing. Indeed, a brother of John Joe, named Jimmy, was killed fighting for Britain at the Somme in World War One.

John Joe told Brian of Jimmy's being attracted to the uniform and the glamour of the recruiting band as it played through the streets of Tralee at the beginning of World War One.[1] As with so many other adventurous young men of the time the pull of the excitement cost Sheehy's brother his life.

And though a strong anti-Imperialist, John Joe could bury his prejudices in exceptional circumstances and could understand the reason for his brother's innocent folly in joining the British Army.

A lifelong friend of his who joined the British Army with Jimmy survived the Battle of the Somme. This man, whom Brian remembered by his nickname, 'Johnny Balnamona', was to accompany the great Kerry Republican, and former Kerry captain, and GAA administrator to many a football match for years to follow.

Sheehy became the spearhead of Republicanism in Kerry in the decades immediately following the Civil War. In the GAA he was to be instrumental in heading off proposals for the removal of the Ban on the playing of foreign games, which eventually was removed from the Rule Book of the GAA at a Congress in Belfast in 1971.

His sisters, Sally and Aggie (married to star Kerry forward Jackie Ryan), were very involved in Cumann na mBan and Sally was one of the good women of Tralee who ventured out to Ballyseedy to collect the remains of the eight Republicans blown up by the Free State Army in the mine atrocity of March 6th/7th, 1923. The Army had not collected all of the pieces of human remains for the nine coffins handed out the Barracks' gate to the mourning relatives and comrades.

Sheehy started work as a porter in Tralee Railway Station as a young man but between being on the run and being hounded out of jobs by unsympathetic governments he was for years unemployed. Republicans found it difficult to get work. He eventually joined the Irish National Insurance Company / New Ireland Assurance Company Ltd. and became a highly successful official with one of the most thriving businesses in the country. He finished his business career as Chief Inspector for the country.

John Joe's political and sporting career makes a most extraordinary story. He played a major part in Kerry's football success story up to his death in 1980 at the age of 83 when he was still President of the Kerry County Board. Of his four All Ireland medals, he won the last as Kerry captain in 1930, the year in which he retired from the game. His football career had been steeped in politics, and his contemporaries would say he was so political and fiery that it took a peacemaker of Con Brosnan's calibre, who also was headstrong, to counterbalance John Joe for the sake of the game which they both loved.

Sheehy spent many years on the run as a prominent IRA man and was actively involved in the War of Independence, the Civil War and eventually in varying capacities in the campaigns that followed. He was interned in the '40s. His son Brian followed his political footsteps and served a sentence in Mountjoy Prison for activities in the late 1950s IRA Border Campaign.

At 19 years of age in 1916 Sheehy had been a Volunteer in the Tralee Battalion when Austin Stack, who had captained Kerry's All Ireland football team in 1904, oversaw the abortive Roger Casement landing with the failed attempt to bring arms in from the German ship, the Aud, in Tralee Bay. Republicans of Tralee had to live down the ignominy of allowing Casement to be arrested in Currahane, Ardfert, to be taken unchallenged by an RIC patrol from Ardfert Barracks to Tralee RIC Barracks. Sir Roger Casement was then taken from Tralee by train before being shipped to London where he was eventually executed by the Crown. According to old Kerry Republicans, this was a source of embarrassment for them throughout their lives.

It would be difficult for Kerry people and especially Tralee townspeople to explain the seemingly bungled attempt to land the arms on Easter Sunday but Niall Harrington in his book Kerry Landing seems to have captured the true account of the events and thus clears Austin Stack, Sheehy and the other Kerry Republicans of the charge of gross inefficiency which was to be levelled at them in the ensuing years.

Harrington's version begins:
"ON EASTER SUNDAY, THE KERRY VOLUNTEERS ASSEMBLED AT THE RINK IN TRALEE TO RECEIVE ORDERS. BUT THE ARMS-BEARING AUD HAD ALREADY COME INTO TRALEE BAY ON HOLY THURSDAY, AND WAS GONE. THE LATE CHANGE IN THE ARRIVAL DATE OF THE SHIPMENT, WHETHER MADE BY THE GERMAN ADMIRALTY OR BY THE SECRET MILITARY COUNCIL OF THE IRB IN DUBLIN, HAD NOT BEEN COMMUNICATED TO AUSTIN STACK." [2]

Historian Fr. Anthony Gaughan in his work, Austin Stack Portrait of a Separatist, lays the blame at the hands of Count

Plunkett. After examining the timing of various messages between the Germans, who were supplying the arms, the Military Council in Dublin and John Devoy in New York, Gaughan eventually blames Plunkett thus:

"IT IS POSSIBLE THAT COUNT PLUNKETT DELIVERED THE MESSAGE AS IT WAS ENTRUSTED TO HIM BY THE MILITARY COUNCIL BUT THIS IS VERY UNLIKELY. IT IS FAR MORE PROBABLE THAT THE COUNT, WHO WAS GENERALLY REGARDED AS RATHER INCOMPETENT, BUNGLED THE MESSAGE. IF ONE, THEREFORE, WERE TO LOOK FOR A SINGLE SCAPEGOAT FOR THE FAILURE OF THE PROPOSED ARMS LANDING IN KERRY, COUNT PLUNKETT WOULD SEEM TO BE THE MOST OBVIOUS CANDIDATE." [3]

As mentioned earlier, in Kerry it is still claimed that the raid on Gortatlea Barracks on April 10, 1918, by an IRA unit led by Tom McEllistrim and Jack Cronin, was the first official action of the War of Independence. Volunteers Browne and Laide lost their lives in that action, which was the first Barracks attack since 1916. It predated Dan Breen's Soloheadbeg ambush of January 21st, 1919 which in fact killed the first two RIC men and in effect is deemed by historians to have begun the War of Independence.

Although the scale of Kerry action was considerably less than the magnitude of Tom Barry's incredible assault on the British Empire in County Cork there was still no shortage of action in Kerry for the duration of the "Troubles". And John Joe Sheehy was deeply involved in many of the most important actions of that time. It was Sheehy as Assistant Commandant of the Tralee Battalion, IRA who planned the shooting of Major MacKinnon on Tralee Golf Course. This was a reprisal for the shooting dead of two Volunteers by MacKinnon on Christmas Eve, 1920, immediately following their capture.

In Uinseann Mac Eoin's - Survivors, John Joe Sheehy described the kind of British soldier MacKinnon was:

"MACKINNON BECAME SO BOLD AND BRAZEN THAT HE WENT AROUND THE COUNTRYSIDE WITH A MACHINE GUN ON HIS SHOULDER. HE WAS A TER-

ROR. IN FACT, ON ONE OF THOSE RAIDS NEAR BALLYMACELLIGOTT, FIVE MILES OUT THE CASTLEISLAND ROAD ON THE LEFT HAND SIDE, HE CALLED TO THIS HOUSE AT BALLYDWYER ON CHRISTMAS NIGHT, 1920. IT WAS THE HOME OF JOHN BYRNE, THE LOCAL CREAMERY MANAGER, A KEY MAN IN THE ORGANISATION AND A BROTHER-IN-LAW OF TOMMY MCELLISTRIM. THERE WERE TWO VOLUNTEERS THERE, MOSSY REIDY AND JOHN LEEN. MACKINNON WENT IN AND SHOT THEM DEAD. THAT IS WHERE THE BALLYMAC POST OFFICE IS NOW. A MYTH GREW UP ABOUT MACKINNON THAT THE LAST WORDS HE SAID (AFTER BEING MORTALLY WOUNDED) WERE BURN BALLYMAC!. BUT IT WAS THE BOHERBEE (TRALEE) SECTION OF THE COLUMN THAT SLEW HIM." [4]

Former IRA man, lifelong Republican, journalist for 48 years, and long time Editor of The Kerryman newspaper, Con Casey, credited Sheehy with the thorough planning of the MacKinnon ambush and was high in his praise for Sheehy's efficient tactics in getting all the IRA personnel away from the area safely by cutting off all the British Army routes to the Golf Course from Tralee.

Casey had once been interrogated, under arrest, by the notorious Major MacKinnon:

"He was a fine soldier. Very brave but utterly ruthless. He would drive around in an open sports type car with a machine gun in his hands. Just to defy the IRA and our sympathisers."

The folly of taking group photographs of Volunteers in the early stages of the War of Independence was brought home to Con Casey during that interrogation when he noticed MacKinnon had a picture of the Boherbee Company of Volunteers in front of him. Casey said Sheehy always claimed "it was the most stupid picture ever taken."

According to Casey, Sheehy believed MacKinnon had to be "eliminated" after he had murdered two Ballymacelligott men, Leen and Reidy, on Christmas Eve 1920. As a result of MacKinnon's shooting less than four months later on April 15th, 1921, the town of Tralee was extensively burned by the

When the twain did meet. Free State Army officer, Jack Higgins, captain of Kildare with former IRA man, Joe Barrett, captain of Kerry and the Bishop of Kildare before the 1929 All Ireland football final.

Five days after Joe Barrett's death, my sister Frances' First Communion called for brave faces. Also in picture: my mother and older brothers, John at back and Tim. The author is pictured left.

A light moment at the home of Kerry star Mikey Sheehy after he had won his first All Ireland in 1975. Three generations of Austin Stack's footballers are represented in the picture, Tommy Barrett of the '20s/'30s, the author '50s/'70s, M. Sheehy '70s/'80s, and Cork All Ireland medal winner, Denis Long, who starred with Austin Stacks in the '70s/'80s.

The breakthrough. Austin Stacks beat West Kerry in the 1973 County Final to win their first championship in 37 years and launch Kerry into a new era in All Ireland suc-

Front row, left to right: Michael McCarthy, Timmy Sheehan, Jo Jo Barrett, Billy Curtin (captain), Gerard O'Keeffe, Tommy Kennington and Gary Scollard.
Back row, left to right: Tommy Rogan, Noel Kelter, Teddy Brick, Ger Power, John O'Keeffe, Anthony O'Keeffe, John Barry and Michael Sheehy.

Kerry Trainer/Manager, Dr. Eamonn O'Sullivan imparts his own extraordinary and most successful brand of psychology at a team talk in Killarney 1962.

Dan McAuliffe receives treatment to an achilles problem from masseur Mick Jennings while receiving ample moral support from team mates.

Captain Peter Trant-Foley, seventh from right at back, with the Officers of the Kerry Militia at the Presentation of Colours in Ballymullen Barracks, Tralee 1904.

The British Army Garrison/Kerry Militia Munster Fusiliers on parade in Tralee, Ballymullen Barracks, in 1904.

Exhumation of Mrs. Hanafin for postmortem purposes as a result of official inquiry into her death.

Margaret Hanafin, who died after being evicted by Landlord, Peter Trant-Foley at Clahane, Tralee.

Paddy Conway and his second wife, and sister outside the doorway of their house where his first wife was shot by Black and Tans.

Mrs. Nora Conway, who was murdered by Black and Tans in Tralee, in May 1921.

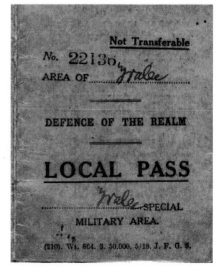

Tim Barrett's local pass for getting to work at O'Donovans Mills, Tralee.

Some ex-internees in training after release in 1924. All Ireland winners, Denis "Rory" O'Connell, John "Gal" Slattery and Jerry "Pluggy" Moriarty are amongst them.

The dilemma of Kerry players is typified in this team picture where 10 ex-internees pose with ex Free State Army Captain, Con Brosnan and Gardai Tim O'Donnell and Paul Russell.

Kerry Team 1929 - start of 4 in a row - five profiled players involved.

The 1926 Kerry hurling team which beat Waterford in Tralee, with Johnny O'Riordan, who was in the ambush party which killed Major MacKinnon. Also included are John Joe Sheehy, Joe Barrett and IRA leader, Humphrey Murphy, who was involved in the planning of the Knocknagoshel Mine, and Jackie Ryan, winner of 6 All Ireland football medals. Alongside Joe Barrett is fellow Rock Street player Gerry "Pluggy" Moriarty, who was involved in the shooting of Constable Benson.

An aerial picture of Fenit Pier showing the distance the troops had to fight their way ashore.

Fenit Pier Viaduct where a mine was defused before the Free State Troop landing in 1922.

John Nolan, who carried the mine on his bicycle to Knocknagoshel.

Picture of Kitty Barrett with her younger sister Vourneen and a friend on a tree, felled by the IRA, at "the Spa".

Kathleen Walsh in the U.S.A.

The shattered stones where the mine
exploded at Barndarrig Wood,
Knocknagoshel. No memorial or cross
marks the spot where the Free State
troops were killed.

Dan Murphy who was shot by Free
State troops as a result of the
Knocknagoshel mine.

Stephen Fuller, in hat, the sole survivor of Ballyseedy mine explosion.

Clashmealcon Monument on the cliffs over-looking the caves and the mouth of Shannon Estuary.

NOTICE.

DEATH SENTENCES.

WHEREAS,

MATTHEW MORONEY, of Boherbee, Tralee;

THOMAS DEVANE, of Dingle;

CORNELIUS CASEY, of Bridge Street, Tralee; and

DERMOT O'CONNOR, of Moyderwell, Tralee,

were each found guilty of having possession, without proper authority, of a Rifle and Ammunition for such Rifle, and were

SENTENCED TO DEATH.

And Whereas the finding and sentence were duly confirmed.

And Whereas the Confirming Authority, influenced by the favourable reports of the G. O. C. Kerry Command, as to the general tendency of the situation in Kerry, has suspended the execution of the sentence in each of these cases on certain conditions.

Notice is hereby given that if after 21st December, 1922, any of the following offences :

(1) Ambushes or attacks on National Troops.

(2) Interference with the Railways or Roads, or

(3) Interference with Private Property,

are committed, the stay on the exection of the sentences will be removed and the sentence of death on each of the above named men will be forthwith carried out.

Dated this 18th day of December, 1922.

W. R. E. MURPHY, C/General,

G. O. C. Kerry Command.

Death Sentence Notice for Con Casey and others.

The Kerry Team of 1929 with the Sam Maguire Cup coming to Kerry for the first time. Kerry were also National League champions at the time. To the extreme left, in sui,t is one of the great peacemakers at the time, County Board Secretary, D.J. Baily.

John Joe Sheehy and his four sons, Paudie, Niall, Brian and Sean Og in 1962 when Sean Og captained Kerry to win the Sam Maguire.

The author with Tim O'Donnell at his 90th birthday party in 1997.

Capt. Con Brosnan in Free State Army uniform outside Moyvane Parish Church during the Civil War.

Extract from Joe Barrett's diary.

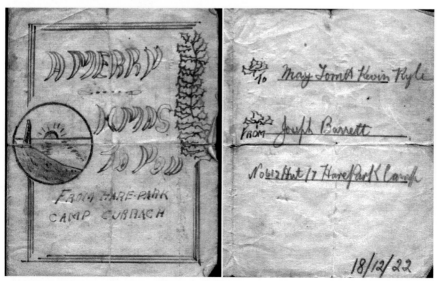

Christmas card from Joe Barrett while interned in Curragh Camp.

Joe Barrett's short fuse in evidence when he became involved in the 1937 All Ireland Final, although then a Kerry selector. Rushing to his aid are Purty Landers, Miko Doyle, Roundy Landers and Charlie O'Sullivan.

A group of the notorious Auxiliaries and Black and Tans whooping it up outside the Eccles Hotel in Glengarriff.

Con Brosnan

John Joe Sheehy

Tim O'Donnell

Johnny Walsh

Joe Barrett

John Joe (Purty) Landers

Charlie Daly,
executed at Drumboe
Castle, Co. Donegal

Brigadier General
Paddy O'Daly

Black and Tans and Auxiliaries. There were many reprisals by the British Forces under a severely enforced curfew for which John Joe Sheehy and the IRA shouldered the blame by non-nationalist sympathisers. It was felt by some that the IRA action in killing the notorious thirty two year old Dumbarton, Scotland-born J.J.A. MacKinnon brought the wrath of the British forces on the people of Tralee. Casey said "this was a fact but it is a price you pay in war."[5]

The reply from the IRA was the shooting of RIC Head Constable Benson in Pembroke Street off Rock Street a month later on May 14th. Sligo born Frank Benson was aged 42 when killed. He had joined the Auxiliaries from the RIC where he had been a District Inspector. [6]

Con Casey was a lifelong friend and near neighbour of Sheehy and in fact he credits Sheehy with saving his life after he was arrested on November 1st 1922 by the Free State Army, he and three other IRA men, Jeremiah (Unkey) O'Connor and Matt Moroney from Tralee, and Tom Devane from Dingle, were under sentence of death. The Notice of Sentence of Death had been posted around the area and the execution of the four hostages arranged to be carried out as a future reprisal and deterrent to IRA actions.

As a counter move, Sheehy sent word to the Tralee Free State Army HQ with a list of twenty well- known Free State sympathisers, including some prominent Tralee business people, would be shot as a reprisal if anything happened the four IRA men. Casey and the other three were, accordingly, spared the firing squad at Ballymullen Barracks, Tralee.

Instead, the four had their sentences commuted to 10 years penal servitude. They were transferred from Tralee Old County Jail to Mountjoy Jail in February 1923. They went on a 44 day hunger strike on which two of Casey's colleagues, Barry of Cork and O'Sullivan from Mallow died. Casey was eventually transferred to Newbridge Barracks, then the Military Hospital and eventually moved to Hare Park, the Curragh, where he saw out the Civil War before his release in June 1924.

I interviewed this 97 year old lifelong Republican about his friendship with John Joe Sheehy, on January 20th, 1996. His extraordinary power of recall, combined with his honest but modest sensitivity, made one realise this was an unrepeatable occasion in the company of a man from a generation sadly lost to this country forever.

The admiration held for Sheehy by his neighbour still glowed as Casey faced almost a century as a Tralee man. He still proudly displayed his grandparents' wedding certificate dated 1819 in Tralee. Casey further enhanced Sheehy's towering reputation when describing how he saved the life of a fellow prisoner, Joe Curtin, as they were both being transported to Limerick Jail by lorry in 1920. A British soldier took Curtin up a side road to shoot him, but, John Joe knew one of the accompanying RIC men who played hurling and Sheehy successfully pleaded with him for Curtin's life. Sheehy was held in Limerick Jail for three months at that time.

By the time the Civil War began in 1922 John Joe Sheehy was one of leaders of the Kerry IRA. It happened that the Tralee IRA was subdivided according to the divisions of the three GAA clubs in the town. Each one represented a fighting Company in the Tralee Battalion area. Sheehy was Commandant of the Tralee Battalion and was also a member of the Kerry senior football team at the same time. As it turned out, those involved in Kerry football were eventually to be mainly responsible for healing the sores of the War amongst brothers. They thus created the real birth of Kerry football in that era directly following the hatred-filled and sadly divisive Civil War.

When the Free State Army invaded Tralee on August 2nd, 1922, after landing at Fenit Port, John Joe Sheehy was in charge of the Tralee IRA section which had commandeered the former British Army barracks at Ballymullen. The invading troops met the heaviest resistance when they encountered the Lewis machine gun operated by Johnny O'Connor from the roof of the Shamrock Mills overlooking Rock Street.

The Free State troops eventually annexed the town but

before retreating Sheehy and his men burned down much of the Ballymullen Army Barracks buildings. Sheehy was wounded in the arm by a Free State bullet at Moyderwell Cross the same day.

The Dublin Guards of the Free State Army which had landed in Fenit Port on that August Monday morning suffered heavy casualties when fighting their way from the port to Tralee Barracks, which was nine miles away. The day left nine young Free State Army soldiers dead, a life for every mile, and two IRA men were killed during the fighting which ensued.

The tragedy of war is sadly underlined when one considers the ages of the young Dublin Guards who fell in the battle to capture the town of Tralee on that sunny August Monday. The youngest was Private James O'Connor of Summerhill who was 17 years, Corporal W D Carson and Privates Patrick Harding and John Kenny, all 19 years, Private Patrick Reilly 22 years, Private Patrick Quinn and Sergeant Fred Gillespie, both 23 years, and Private Thomas Larkin and Corporal Michael Farrell, both 27 years.[7]

My mother has good reason to recall the day of the landing as she lived on the Fenit to Tralee road. She and her sister were playing on the road about fifty yards from the house when the advancing troops under Captain Billy McLean appeared. At eighty five she still remembers Captain McLean picking up the two children and carrying them to the safety of their home. Kitty also sadly remembers the keening of local mother, Mrs Flynn, taking home her dead son, Volunteer Tom, to Kilfenora, near Fenit, in a donkey's cart that day.

The real history of the Civil War in Kerry began on that sunny August Monday morning. Fenit was a thriving Port at the time but went very close to being wiped off the map as a commercial base for the area on that day. The timber viaduct out to the port from the mainland would have to be crossed by the invading troops. The IRA had mined the viaduct in case of a landing. The mine was made by Tadhg Kelliher of Tralee. However, two local men with the commercial well-being of the area at heart, neutralised the mine. The mine wire was cut by Danny King and Ned Sheehan and thus the life of Kerry's main port had a miraculous escape as the viaduct was the lifeline for all transport to the port. It even carried the railway line down to the quayside. Though the port was saved, this action also allowed the Free State troops ashore. For Republicans it was a disaster, for Fenit it was a near miracle in times when jobs were not easily found in the area. The thriving port provided scores of jobs for dockers.

A picture of the author's mother, Kitty, and sister Vourneen and a young friend, Betty Deanrow, standing on a felled tree outside her home at The Spa on the Fenit to Tralee road. The felling of trees was a common IRA tactic to hamper efficient troop mobility during the Civil War.

The Civil War left many memories of terrible deeds but also of outstanding acts of bravery on both sides in Kerry history following the Civil War. One such account is of a day when John Joe Sheehy saved his company of IRA men during an ambush in the Scartaglen area when they were pinned down. Sheehy broke away and encircled the machine gun nest from where the damage was coming. Soon after, the Free State guns fell silent. Naturally, one must realise that accounts of such events were not spoken of, or were certainly played down for decades. Killing during the Civil War was rarely attributed to individuals. The nature of a civil war demanded a silence if life was to return to normal.

I asked Con Casey if this incident in Scartaglen happened and he replied knowingly, "It was possible indeed!"

Three years after the Civil War John Joe Sheehy had another term in jail in the twenties when he, Con Casey and John Joe Rice, all leading Republicans, were taken to Mountjoy for three weeks in 1926. It was the same year as Sheehy won his second All Ireland football medal as he captained Kerry to beat Kildare 1-4 to 0-4 in a thrilling replay. The replay of the All Ireland Final was also the game in which Dr. Eamonn O'Sullivan took over as trainer of the Kerry team. So began a long football relationship between John Joe Sheehy and the Doc., which culminated in O'Sullivan training the successful Kerry team of 1962 when three of John Joe Sheehy's sons, Niall, Paudi and team captain, Sean Og, were on the winning team against Roscommon. John Joe himself was a member of the selection committee. That year saw the total All Ireland Senior football medal tally rise to eleven for the Sheehy household.

Throughout the 1920s Sheehy retained his active involvement with the IRA and when Eamon De Valera was forming the Fianna Fail Party in 1927 he tried to invoke the cooperation and assistance of Sheehy and Austin Stack as representatives of the Republican Movement in Kerry. De Valera's attempt failed.

A further All Ireland medal in 1929 and another successful captaincy in 1930 saw the end of Sheehy's inter-county career at the age of 33, having first played with Kerry in 1919.

Trips to the USA with Kerry teams during his playing career incredibly saw Sheehy organise players of varying political beliefs smuggle a quantity of Thompson machine guns back to Ireland with their football gear. It was unspoken of in the history of Kerry football, but happened all the same.

During those tense political playing years the singularly Republican-minded Sheehy had shared the Kerry colours with men with whom he was politically polarly opposed. He played alongside Gardai, Free Staters and men of very differing ideals to his own. Through the Blueshirt era of the early thirties and on towards the IRA campaign of the forties he was still a committed Republican and was a prominent Kerry County GAA Board and Munster GAA Council Official.

He reared a fine family, though widowed with six children in 1948. It was he who organised the fundraising for the Ballyseedy Monument. Indeed, in all that time he was totally immersed in Kerry's football story with his inspiring contribution. John Joe Sheehy died as President of the Kerry GAA. He had never deviated from his National ideals and when he did relent to those of opposing beliefs it was for the good of Gaelic games and his county.

Carbery summed up John Joe's contribution as Kerry Captain as follows:

"JOHN JOE SHEEHY OF BOHERBEE, TRALEE - ONE OF OUR GREATEST GAELIC CAPTAINS. IMAGINE A WELL PROPORTIONED MAN OF 5-11, WEIGHING 13.5 STONE, ALWAYS IN THE PINK OF CONDITION, OF ACTIVE AND ABSTEMIOUS LIFE, SPEED OF 100 YARDS MAN, AND ALL THE FOOTBALL ART OF THE BEST TRALEE SCHOOL - IMAGINE HIM IN ALL THE EXUBERANCE OF HEFTY VIRILE MANHOOD, TEARING IN AT THE HEAD OF A PACK OF RESOLUTE KERRY FORWARDS. THAT WAS JOHN JOE SHEEHY, CAPTAIN OF WINNING KERRY TEAMS IN THEIR BEST YEARS. A MAN OF HIGH MENTAL ATTRIBUTES, HE WAS A DOMINANT FORCE AROUND THE 1924 TO 1931 PERIOD. HE SHOULD HAVE WON SEVEN ALL IRELANDS INSTEAD OF FOUR BEFORE HE RETIRED. HE HAD ALL THE SKILL OF THE LANDERS AND BAILEYS IN ATTACK- HIS SHOT WOULD BORE A HOLE THROUGH A GOAL NET AND DID WHEN TWAS NOT KEPT IN SOUND REPAIR. HE WAS A LEADER IN COUNSEL AND CLUB, AN IMPRESSIVE SPEAKER, HE ALWAYS KEPT HIGH NATIONAL PRINCIPLES. FOREMOST IN THE FIGHT FOR FREEDOM, HE HAS SUFFERED MANY TERMS OF IMPRISONMENT, YET HIS VIGOUR AND FRESH MENTALITY IS BUOYANT AS EVER. HE WAS A FINE HURLER, SELECTED FOR MUNSTER. I LIKE TO REMEMBER HIM AS LEFT WING, "FORTY MAN", OR CORNER - HE PULLED GAMES OUT OF THE FIRE, A DOZEN COUNTY, NINE MUNSTER, FOUR NATIONAL LEAGUES, INTERNATIONAL HONOURS - ALL CAME TO HIM. HE COULD DOUBLE TURN ON A PLATE-UNUSUAL FOR SUCH A BIG MAN, HIS RISING SHOT DEAD ON MARK HAD THE FORCE OF A CANNON BALL. ONE OF KERRY'S FINEST FOOTBALLERS AND NOBLE, UNCOMPROMISING IRISHMEN." [8]

The road which runs by the Kerry GAA HQ at Austin Stack Park, Tralee, is officially named John Joe Sheehy Road in a fitting tribute to an outstanding Irishman.

During his last fatal illness, I visited him at the Bon Secour Hospital, Tralee. Although his time on this earth was running out quickly, his interest in Kerry football was as strong as ever.

Chapter 7

Johnny Walsh of Ballylongford

Of the bridge builders we are profiling, the experience of the youngest of our personalities, Johnny Walsh, of Ballylongford is worth recalling. Because of his age, Johnny was not involved in the War of Independence or the Civil War. But because he later held very strong political views his story is worth recalling to further emphasise the reconciliatory nature of that era in Kerry football. Johnny won five All Ireland medals with Kerry up to 1941.

His sons Jackie and Barry won All Ireland medals as members of the star laden Kerry squad of the 1970s, into the '80s. They also won Kerry County Championship medals as they followed in the footsteps of their highly motivated father.

In his own illustrious and colourful playing career Johnny Walsh was another star who, along with Purty Landers, linked the glorious four-in-a-row of 1929 to 1932 and the four out of five titles won from 1937 to 1941. His political beliefs would have been directly and stridently opposed to those of Purty Landers' Rock Street Club and yet when this great North Kerry footballer had given up the game for a successful few years in Munster Senior Rugby, it was Rock Club star (Austin Stack's Club) colleague Miko Doyle who travelled out the 26 long miles in the bad roads of those times to Walsh's home in Ballylongford to convince him to make a return to Gaelic football.

Walsh, as a 21 year old, won his first All Ireland medal when Kerry completed their four-in-a-row in 1932. But now four years later Kerry football was going through a bad political period.

It was 1936 and after a few over politicised years in the Kingdom they badly needed another All Ireland title and Johnny Walsh would be a great boon to their chances. The ban on GAA players playing foreign games was very much in operation. If only he would seek reconciliation with the Kerry County Board and terminate his involvement with Limerick's famous Garryowen Rugby Club.

As stated, Walsh was totally opposed to the IRA. The iron man from Ballylongford had taken on the IRA in his home town when they had stuck Easter Lily posters and Republican slogans on Johnny's father's business premises. The Kerry player, a local national teacher, took on a group of active IRA men and ripped down every poster they attempted to paste on his wall. This led to a confrontation which will be later described in this chapter. It also almost led to a riot in the town of Ballylongford which necessitated the calling for Garda reinforcements from Listowel, which is a good nine miles from where Walsh was under siege. The sheer doggedness and courage displayed by the Ballylongford school master on that occasion was against the political beliefs of Purty Landers but when it came to improving the lot of Kerry football, and when it was seen as imperative that Johnny Walsh come back into the Kerry football fold, then Purty and Johnny would bury their political differences. Purty's Austin Stack's club mate Miko Doyle was seen as the person to send on the delicate mission of the reconversion of the granite-like Walsh.

Johnny was a man of immovable principles. He was also a man of powerful strength, stern courage, a very short fuse, great football knowledge and devotion to the Kerry colours. When Miko Doyle faced Ballylongford to try talking Walsh back into Kerry service he knew Walsh as one of the hardest men in the field of play, and that he would be crucial to the success of Kerry football over the next five or so years. History proved him right, for Walsh went on to win his fifth All Ireland football medal in 1941.

Johnny could always, also, be counted on to look after his younger colleagues in a team being rebuilt and so, at 25 years of age, in 1936 when he was asked to seek reinstatement to the Kerry jersey, having been suspended under Rule 27 for playing foreign games, Walsh gave Miko a positive answer and was back in the multi partied political Kerry football scene again.

The author has known Johnny Walsh since 1960 when, as a young player he first came into contact with the then Kerry selector. Travelling to matches in the same car was always a great pleasure. Over the years I saw many sides to Johnny Walsh, not one of which I didn't like. So to include the Ballylongford Master in these profiles adds much of the spice and flavour for which Kerry football was once renowned. I have seen the toughest side of Walsh and I have seen a soft side too. I can even go back to the All Ireland Final of 1959 when Johnny's short fuse led him to take issue with Galway mid-fielder, Frank Evers after the All Ireland Final. Johnny was a Kerry selector and Frank had been dishing out some heavy tackling to Mick O'Connell during the game.

There are many stories could be told about Johnny's years as a Kerry selector and any player who shared those five-person cars to all parts of the 32 Counties in his company will vouch for the enjoyment and good humour he brought with him when on occasions collected by the Tralee car at his bar. He often started us out on our journey in a much lighter mood as a result of his hospitality at his pub on the main street of the North Kerry town. As for coming home on Sunday night, that was another story.

When I visited Johnny at his home to do an interview for this book I saw how mellow he had become over the years and his awareness of old age and good days spent together in the distant past brought a tear or two to eyes of the old lion.

On a lighter note about this extraordinary son of a Clonakilty, County Cork man, David Walsh, who moved to Ballylongford as Creamery Manager in 1909. It was in 1994 that I was one morning driving my son Joe to Sean Heuston Station in Dublin when I saw fellow Kerryman and famous poet, Brendan Kennelly going for a walk along South Circular Road. I stopped to bid the time of day with the Ballylongford man and he relaxed into the back seat for a chat for a few minutes.

I, of course asked him how his neighbour and former teacher, Johnny Walsh, was getting on. Brendan replied: "Still hitting, at 84. Sure he's fine, thank God."

Johnny Walsh was born in 1911. He was educated at Ballylongford NS and Rockwell College. As a teenager his hero was Con Brosnan and to this day nothing in his long life has changed that respect for his friend from the neighbouring North Kerry village of Moyvane (formerly Newtownsandes). At age 21, in 1932, he joined one of the greatest Kerry teams in history to win his first All Ireland, as Kerry completed their four in a row. It was Joe Barrett's second successful All Ireland winning captaincy and on that side Johnny had teamed up with his idol, Con Brosnan, Jack Walsh, Bob Stack, Jacky Ryan and Paul Russell, all of whom were winning their record sixth senior All Ireland medal.

The following year Kerry football was rocked to the core once more when the Blueshirt Movement under Eoin O'Duffy tested the capacity of many Kerry footballers to play side by side. Some vigorously supported O'Duffy's ideals, others were polarly opposed to the explosive Blueshirt Movement. Johnny Walsh was an avid Cumann na nGaedheal supporter and strong admirer of Con Brosnan, who was one of the standard bearers of the Cumann na nGaedheal Party in North Kerry.

The "Siamese Twins" relationship between The Blueshirts and Cumann na nGaedheal meant both organisations were being opposed by the Fianna Fail Government and the IRA. These two organisations were also going through a steadily declining relationship which eventually saw the De Valera-led Government outlaw and imprison the IRA.

It was a difficult time to control one's political passion. For people like Johnny Walsh and Con Brosnan it must have been painfully distressing to steer a course through the political morass without offending many GAA colleagues who would be so stridently opposed to their political party philosophy. In actual fact, Brosnan had major misgivings about where the Blueshirt movement was going and he resigned from it.

At Easter 1933 an incident happened in Ballylongford which alienated the young Kerry footballer from many of his more Republican-minded friends inside and outside of football.

Walsh felt his household had been subjected to much harassment during the stormy elections as bonfires burned outside their door and slogans appeared close to their home. Even in the author's time in the '50s, the winners of elections would goad the opposition by lighting bonfires close to the homes of the beaten party members.

On Good Friday Walsh became aware of a group of three active Republican sympathisers attempting to paint slogans on Walsh's house, advocating the purchase of Easter Lilies. Walsh charged out and unceremoniously convinced the people involved of their folly. This was, of course, not the end of the episode and a party of 40 IRA sympathisers returned later in military formation to impose their will on the brave but reckless young Kerry player. Unperturbed by the show of strength, Walsh faced the Republicans with a hurley, while his only supporter, Mike Moynihan, was armed with an iron bar. A skirmish ensued before the Gardai arrived but the local force had to call for reinforcements from Listowel before order was restored to the town. Walsh was arrested but never charged and to this day he jokes about the incident : "It was the only time I ever caught a hurley."

Word of this incident spread and Walsh was dubbed a Blueshirt, as was the universal identity of all Cumann na nGaedheal followers at the time. Indeed, in some places it is used to identify in a derogatory way the Fine Gael Party, even to the present day.

The year 1933 also saw Johnny tour the USA with the Kerry team and when he lined out with the Kingdom in the Polo Grounds, New York, his deeds of the previous Easter were to come back to haunt him. In Walsh's own words:

"I got hit very hard in the first ball I went for. I was really hurt and Bob Stack came over to me and said, You left yourself open there, Johnny." [9]

Kerry had only landed off an Ocean Liner on the previous Thursday and so Walsh believes they hadn't got rid of their sea legs by Sunday. Walsh further describes what happened next.

"I really wasn't tall enough to play midfield in a small pitch and so they switched me to wing forward onto a tough bully named Armitage. The first thing he said was: You Blueshirt, I'll send you back to Cosgrave in a coffin." (William Cosgrave, President of Executive Council, an office later renamed as Taoiseach, and Cumann na nGaedheal Party leader. He was leader of the government from 1922 to 1932).

Johnny replied: "You have an hour to do it." Walsh had boxed as a student in University College Dublin and had a good idea of what to do next. He hit the New York player with his fist:

"I saw his eyes rolling in his head, and just before half-time I pretended to go down for a ball and Armitage came for me again. He broke three of his ribs and New York then brought in a sub. When the sub arrived he admitted to Johnny;

"I don't like dirty play."

"I don't either," said Walsh, and so a certain peace broke out between them.

Johnny's account of that match was recalled with no sparing of his old sparring partner Armitage. However, the distinguished Gaelic Games writer "Carbery", thought very highly of Armitage as a player. This account which was written in 1947:

"TOMMY ARMITAGE WAS AMERICA'S MOST FAMOUS CAPTAIN. BORN IN TEMPLEMORE IN 1902 HE STILL PLAYS A GOOD GAME AT 45 THOUGH WEIGHING OVER 16 STONE. THE TIPPERARY MAN STOOD 5FT 10 AND WEIGHED 14.5 IN HIS PRIME. HE LEARNED HIS FOOTBALL IN NORTH TIPPERARY, WINNING JUNIOR ALL IRELAND IN 1923 AND SENIOR COUNTY TITLES. BUT IT WAS IN AMERICA HE MADE HIS BIG NAME WITH THE TIPPERARYMENS' TEAM. HE CAPTAINED THAT POWERFUL AMERICAN SIDE IN TAILTEANN GAMES IN 1928 AND 1932. HE LED THOSE NEW YORK WORLD BEATERS WHO PLAYED AND WON AGAINST KERRY, MAYO, CAVAN AND GALWAY SIDES BETWEEN 1930 AND 1934. A BIG BURLEY FIGURE ON THE FIELD, HE WAS FAST, STRONG, AND FEARLESS - RECKONED THE GAMEST, BRIGHTEST STAR DURING HIS PLAYING YEARS."

The clash of these two men in 1934 must have sent shock-waves around New York. However, one thing certain was that Walsh's political beliefs had travelled across the Atlantic before him. Back home, they were to probably cost him his place on the Kerry team the following year. Johnny still believed so himself anyway.

It was a time when Republicans of all persuasions had one common enemy, that of the Blueshirt Movement. Fianna Fail were in power under Eamonn De Valera and the new Government was being tested by both General Eoin O'Duffy (Blueshirt Leader) and the IRA on a daily basis. To this day Johnny Walsh believes the divisiveness of the period cost him his place on the Kerry team of 1934. Kerry played host to Dublin in the All Ireland Semi-Final in Tralee and Johnny Walsh was dropped for the game.

"I was dropped because of my politics," Walsh said.

Kerry lost to Dublin and Walsh departed in disgust to play Rugby with Garryowen. Coincidentally, that game against Dublin was to be Joe Barrett's last match with Kerry, as he retired at the age of 32.

With the Civil War atrocities still fresh in the minds of Kerry Republicans, there was a fierce resistance to the growing Blueshirt movement. For people like Walsh and Brosnan in the Kingdom, this period was to prove another testing time for their loyalty to Kerry football. When General O'Duffy came to Tralee to speak at a public meeting of the Blueshirts there was a riot in the capital town of County Kerry. Many strong Kerry GAA people were amongst the rioting crowd who prevented O'Duffy from speaking or addressing the meeting. It was for long a proud boast of Kerry Republicans that their county was the only one in which O'Duffy failed to hold a successful public meeting.

In his book, The Blueshirts, Maurice Manning details the happenings of that fateful day in Tralee Town.

"ON OCTOBER 6TH, THE WORST DISTURBANCES TO DATE TOOK PLACE AT A MEETING ADDRESSED BY O'DUFFY IN TRALEE. THE MEETING WAS COMPLETELY WRECKED AND O'DUFFY RECEIVED A NASTY HEAD WOUND WHEN HIT WITH A HAMMER ON THE WAY TO THE MEETING. LATER, OVER A HUNDRED FINE GAEL DELEGATES WERE BESIEGED IN A HALL BY A STONE-THROWING CROWD OUTSIDE. THE 200 POLICE PRESENT WERE UNABLE TO DEAL WITH THE CROWD, AND IT WAS NOT UNTIL SOLDIERS, DRESSED IN FULL BATTLE-KIT, ARRIVED FROM CORK AFTER NINE O'CLOCK, THAT PEACE WAS RESTORED. A MILLS BOMB WAS THROWN THROUGH THE SKY-LIGHT OVER THE STAGE, BUT IT DID NOT EXPLODE AS IT WAS CAUGHT IN THE WIRE NETTING." [10]

O'Duffy's car was burned at the rear of the National Bank of Ireland, Denny Street, by a group led by Denis Cotter. O'Duffy and his number two, Comdt. Cronin had to be escorted to the county border by a large police escort. The following day an unexploded bomb was found at the rear of the hall.

Tralee had given the Blueshirt movement its reaction in no uncertain manner, but De Valera's Government was to take stern action against a number of young Tralee Republicans. The Kerry GAA was to suffer accordingly. Amongst the leading lights in the rioting crowd were a number of young footballers from the town and some of the arrests followed would cause many rifts once more amongst the footballing fraternity of the county.

In my profile on John Joe 'Purty' Landers in this book, he gives a thorough and accurate account of that fateful Sunday afternoon on October 6th in 1933. He also named Plumber Kerins as the person who struck O'Duffy with the hammer. Contrary to Maurice Manning's account of the October 6th incidents, Landers is adamant that there was no public meeting held and that General O'Duffy never got a chance to address the abortive Blueshirt gathering in Tralee.

It was after these tense times and under such circumstances that Johnny Walsh was asked by Miko Doyle to return to help out Kerry in 1936, when a major effort was being made to once more, in another decade, set politics aside and concentrate on bringing the Sam Maguire Cup back to Kerry after an absence of four years.

Kerry had stood down from participation in the 1935 Munster Championships in solidarity with a number of Kerry Republicans who were in custody. The team was back in action again in 1936 but after winning the Munster Championship they were beaten by Mayo by 1-5 to 0-6 in the All Ireland Semi-Final, played in Roscommon.

So, at 26 years of age, and after playing in two Munster Rugby Cup Finals with Garryowen, and representing Munster at Interprovincial level, Johnny Walsh was back with the Kerry team which beat Cavan by 4-4 to 1-7 in the replayed All Ireland Final of 1937 in front of a then record crowd of 52,000. [11]

The records tumbled to Walsh's career over the following years. He was on the Kerry team beaten by Galway in controversial circumstances in front of 70,000 people. Then in 1939 and 1940 he went on to collect his third and fourth All Ireland medals. Playing in his fifth consecutive All Ireland Final in 1941, at wing forward, Johnny Walsh won his fifth All Ireland medal, an eventful and at times turbulent nine years after collecting his first honour in 1932.

Much water had flowed under the bridge of Johnny Walsh's life in that golden but highly divisive decade in the history of this country, and in the history of Kerry football. Johnny had been tested on the pitch and never found wanting. His principles had been severely tested and not found wanting either. He could quite easily have walked away for ever from Kerry football when the rugby career at Garryowen called out to him. But, when Kerry decided to put politics aside and asked Johnny Walsh back, he buried his pride and personal hurt for the sake of Kerry football.

In December 1995 the wheel of history completed the full circle for Johnny Walsh when he was unanimously elected President of the Kerry County Board of the GAA.

Chapter 8

John Joe (Purty) Landers

Lifelong Republican and Kerry forward star, John Joe (Purty) Landers, believed football was the saving of Kerry at a time when the evil of the Civil War burrowed deeply into the hearts of neighbour who fought neighbour, and brother who fought brother.

Of the post Civil War traumatic twenties and thirties as an IRA man, with Gardai, and at times Blueshirts, both deadly enemies of Republicanism, and on the same Kerry teams together, Purty explained: "We were likely to shoot at each other all week long and play football together on Sunday."

Purty Landers was the biggest name in Kerry football to be interned during World War Two. His sporting prowess was further confirmed when he became boxing champion of the Curragh Internment Camp when in his thirties. His description of his arrest shows the divided society in which he lived in Kerry in those decades leading up to 1940. He had won five All Ireland senior football medals, had been Secretary of the Kerry County Board and was one of the great folk heroes of that golden era of the '20s and '30s of Kerry football. His political leanings were clearly Republican but his respect for those in football who opposed him politically shines through even to the day of interviewing him in 1995.

Born in Rock Street, Tralee in 1907 John Joe (Purty) Landers was reared in a staunchly Republican area of the town. He was eventually to become one of the leading Republicans in the county over the following decades of upheaval following the Civil War. Even as Kerry County Board Secretary in the thirties he was an active Republican during the Blueshirt era, and the IRA campaign of the late thirties and early forties when he was again interned.

First of all, of course, he was to make an incomparable name for himself as one of the greatest forwards the Kingdom ever produced and was generally accepted by even his political opponents as a man of great honour and integrity. He was a Fianna Boy during the Civil War in Tralee when these youngsters played a major part in reconnaissance and surveillance for their more adult Republican brethren. His older brother Bill was interned during the Civil War.

Rising up above the town on the northern side of Tralee and carrying the Abbeydorney road on towards Ballyduff and Ballybunion stands Bullock Hill. It was here the Rock Street Brigade was billeted and based its operations against the various considered enemies of the turbulent two decades in question from 1920 to 1940. It was up here above Rock Street within a range of one to three miles of the town that Purty Landers spent many years on the run and from which many of his fellow Rock Street team and club colleagues operated their IRA activities. Only coming down for matches of importance under the constant threat of arrest and imprisonment and fading back into the hillsides when matches were over.

In a street which had produced a number of Kerry players from the internment camps of the Civil War, Purty learned his Republicanism and his football in the one pitch. Jerry (Pluggy) Moriarty, Jackie Ryan, Denis (Rory) O'Connell, his brother Bill Landers, John Gal Slattery, Dan Ryan, and Joe Barrett were seasoned campaigners in football and political terms when young Landers first came into the Kerry team as a 20 year old in 1927. It was a year when Kerry lost the All Ireland Final to Kildare by the incredibly low scoreline of 0-5 to 0-3. There were six Republican Rock Street men on that team - Joe Barrett, Denis (Rory) O'Connell, John (Gal) Slattery, Jackie Ryan (later to play with John Mitchel's), James Baily and John Joe Landers - which also included other Tralee IRA men, John Joe Sheehy and Johnny O'Riordan of John Mitchel's. It was also the year Minister Kevin O'Higgins was killed by the IRA in Booterstown Avenue and the political climate throughout the country was on a knife edge.

The following year saw Landers win his first All Ireland medal as Kerry began their four-in-a-row. This glorious run of wins culminating in 1932 as Purty's younger brother Tim (Roundy) collected his second medal after being in as a teenager in 1931. The Landers brothers were household names throughout the game as a most lethal attacking duo and in fact three of the family won All Irelands in '32 as older brother Bill had returned to come in as a substitute. But the political ideal was never far from their minds and Purty described the tension between the various political factions in the Kerry dressing room at that time as "most uncomfortable."

"Sometimes it was so bad that members of the other side in our team would come to a game already togged out." [12]

Kildare and Kerry held a special relationship at that time. Kildare won the title and the inaugural Sam Maguire Cup in 1928. The following year Kerry took it from them when Joe Barrett was captain, the first of the four in a row. The games were hard and though there were a number of Free State Army members on the Kildare side, this political difference was never brought into the contest. However difficult this is to believe, Purty Landers vouched for it as a fact.

Landers said: "Two of the top Kildare players, Jack Higgins and Matt Gough, were Army men but that was never a consideration. Though Gus Fitzpatrick, who was a strong Republican and the only Republican on the Kildare team, spent quite a lot of time with us, because as an IRA man he didn't feel that acceptable amongst his own team mates who were mostly Free State Government supporters."

In Kerry the ratio was different. For example in the 1929 team there were seven Republicans, two Gardai, Tim O'Donnell and Paul Russell, and some very strong Free State sympathisers in Con Brosnan and Bob Stack. Another North Kerry man, Jack Walsh of Craughdarrig, who won six All Ireland medals, was a very close friend of Brosnan and Stack, though he was politically neutral.

"The uneasy atmosphere would be just too much for us to make small talk and socialise with some of the other players. Once we got out onto the pitch everything changed and we knew each other's play so well that the game flowed along and Kerry football amazingly thrived." Purty acknowledged that there was no hugging or kissing of each other after one scored a goal or a point. Politics apart though, that terrible habit we see nowadays, was unheard of in our time.

At 25 Purty had played in five All Ireland Finals but his football career was to go through an erratic curve line over the next five years as his IRA activities, Kerry's stand-downs in 1933 and 1935, and the political divisions of Kerry football caused upheavals which disrupted the progress of the game in the Kingdom.

On October 6th, 1933 an incident was to occur in Tralee which rocked the Kerry GAA to its foundations. An open air public meeting of the Blueshirts was arranged for The Square in Tralee. However, a huge contingent of Republicans from all over the county converged on the North Kerry town and prevented the meeting from taking place.

Prominent Republican Purty Landers described the scenes as General Eoin O'Duffy and Commandant Ned Cronin were being escorted down Bridge St. after the initial attempt to hold the public meeting had failed:

"Fighting was going on all over the place and a few of the younger fellows got close enough for Plumber Kerins to connect with a hammer on O'Duffy's head outside McQuinn's Butcher Shop. There was consternation as a few hundred guards failed to protect the Blueshirt leaders."

Although Purty was sure it was Kerins who struck O'Duffy, another Tralee Republican, Tomo Costello, thought it was Gerry O'Callaghan who used the hammer. In the mayhem that followed, details may have suffered. Landers continued:

"The Blueshirts made their way another 100 yards to The Foresters Hall in Staughtons Row where they tried to hold a meeting under a barrage of stones and other missiles. A grenade was thrown at the hall but failed to explode and O'Duffy's car was burned at the back of Denny St." [12]

Eighty two year old Tomo Costello witnessed the riot of that October day and the eventual burning of O'Duffy's car by Austin Stack's club man Denis Cotter that night. [13]

In Maurice Manning's book it was stated that a bomb was discovered at the back of the (Foresters) Hall [14] on the following day but according to local Republican, John Friday O'Callaghan, the bomb incident was a few years later and was on a night in 1939 when the son of a British Prime Minister, Neville Chamberlain, was holidaying in Hawney's Hotel attached to the Foresters Hall.

A number of Tralee Republicans, all members of one or other of the three Tralee GAA clubs (Austin Stack's, John Mitchel's and O'Rahilly's), were arrested after the Tralee riot. Amongst those arrested were were Sean Ryan, Paddy Curran, Richie Eager, Jack Parker, Merse Foley, Jack Healy, and Jimmy O'Flaherty of Lixnaw. But detained still in Mountjoy Prison in February 1934 were John Joe McMahon, Gerry O'Callaghan, Bernard O'Connor, George Teahan, Eddie O'Sullivan, Jerry Lynch, Johnny Duggan, Florence (Plumber) Kerins and Sean Ryan. [15]

The Kerry County Board held countless protest meetings and matches were unplayed as the continuing imprisonment of these nine GAA men was most strongly opposed by the majority of Kerry people.

"Only for Con Brosnan and Den Joe Bailey, Kerry football could have died a death during those years," said Landers.

"As Kerry Chairman, and though having leanings towards the Government, Den Joe smothered the effects of politics in Kerry football as best he could. He was a great Chairman."

According to Landers: "There were plenty of people who would have used Kerry football to further their political aims but Brosnan and Bailey often outwitted them by steering a neutral course without causing a serious confrontation."

In the biography of Eamon De Valera by The Earl of

Longford and Thomas P. O'Neill they underlined the difficult situation in which the Fianna Fail Government found itself at the time. "De Valera had no sympathy with the Blueshirts - he looked on them simply as a body without roots whose sole object was to oust him from office. For the IRA he had greater understanding, although he objected vehemently then and later to their methods." [16]

Kerry hadn't won a title for four years from 1932 when Purty was convinced to make a comeback to the inter-county scene in 1937 at the age of thirty. He had starred for Austin Stack's as they won the Kerry County Championship in 1936.

After two barren years of Kerry football when no County Championship was decided due to the political stand-downs Landers played a major part at full-forward as Austin Stack's overcame another Tralee Club, O'Rahilly's (Strand Road) to win the 1936 Final by 0-6 to 0-4. Midfielders Tim (Roundy) Landers and young Jimmy (Gawksy) Gorman were pitted against the Kerry stars Paddy Kennedy and Dan Spring in that decider.

Purty collected his fifth All Ireland medal in '37 and went in as a sub in 1938 when Kerry were beaten in the Final by Galway as he appeared in his sixth and last All Ireland Final. Against Cavan in the drawn All Ireland Final, Landers scored two first half goals which saw Kerry 2 goals to 0-4 ahead at half time. But at the end of the game, amidst great controversy, a draw of 2-5 to 1-8 was announced, although many Cavan folk believed they had won by a point. A point by Boylan, one of the most debated points in the history of the game, had been disallowed for throwing. In the replay Landers was again on target for another two goals as Kerry took the Championship by 4-4 to 1-7.

Landers believes he had plenty of football left in him at that stage as Kerry collected two more All Irelands in '39 and '40. But those years proved some of the bleakest of his life when a series of arrests for his IRA activities kept him very much out of circulation.

Tralee was a hive of IRA activity in the late thirties, with each of the three football club areas, Rock Street, Strand Road and Boherbee, boasting a company of over 100 Volunteers. In the Easter Parade of 1938 over 100 hundred men from the Boherbee, John Mitchel's Club area, marched from Tralee Sportsfield (GAA) to join up with the other two clubs, with over 100 each at Denny Street. This was the tense atmosphere in which Gaelic football and hurling were played by men of all the varying shades of green in Kerry.

A brief period of freedom after a time in Arbour Hill in 1939 was followed by three and half years in the Curragh Internment Camp until his release in 1943. The description of his arrest before that long incarceration shows the confused political climate of the country at that time.

After being arrested from his bed in the early hours of the morning, Purty was taken to Tralee Garda Barracks where upon arrival he was put in a cell with Strand Road footballers Dan Joe Conway and Richie Eager, and other Republicans (Terry Myles, John Friday O'Callaghan, Dick Cusack, Willie Hobbert, Eugene Powell, Gerry O'Callaghan, Tomo Costello and Willie Walsh of Lixnaw).

Later that night they were joined in their cell by Sean Fuller of Kilflynn. He was a brother of Ballyseedy survivor Stephen Fuller. It is ironic that they were now being arrested and thrown in jail by a Fianna Fail Government then led by Eamon De Valera, for whom Stephen Fuller almost gave his life when fighting for De Valera's side during the Civil War. Stephen Fuller later became a Fianna Fail T.D. for a time.

John Joe (Purty) Landers lives in the loving care of his wife and family in St. Brendan's Park, Tralee. By coincidence, across the road from "Purty", another star forward of a more recent era, Mikey Sheehy, winner of eight All Ireland medals, was reared. At 90 years of age, Purty's eventful life now drifts quietly to a close. He was one of the very colourful and endearing names in the most turbulent two decades in the history of Gaelic football. He never sought the limelight that inevitably found him. His quiet but magnificent contribution to country and county is now, I hope, acknowledged in these pages, whether one agreed with him politically or not.

In the Name of the Game

Chapter 9
Tim O'Donnell

An example of the soul searching done by many people in Kerry in those turbulent decades was the dilemma in which Garda Tim O'Donnell of West Kerry found himself when on December 1st, 1944 Taoiseach Eamon de Valera refused to reprieve from the death sentence IRA man Charlie Kerins of Tralee.

It was a harrowing time for many Gardai who were reared in Republican families, with Padraig Pearse, James Connolly and Michael Collins, Eamon de Valera as their heroes. Twenty six year old Tralee man, Kerins had been convicted by a Military Tribunal of complicity in the shooting dead of Detective Sergeant Dinny O'Brien. The dead detective had a fine record of IRA service during the War of Independence and his brother was, at the time of the killing, Secretary to Government Minister, Sean Lemass. As Kerins did not recognise the Military Court, there was no defence and there were grave doubts as to the verdict and death sentence at which the court arrived. Torn between their loyalty to the force and their love for their native county, the Kerry Gardai, like Tim O'Donnell, went through a heartbreaking time of personal turmoil and indecision.

Having been a prominent Kerry footballer with three All Ireland medals (injury deprived him of '31 and '32), O'Donnell was more conspicuous than others. The divisions which had been healed to a considerable extent after the Civil War in Kerry were to come very close to the surface in Kerry life again in the forties when many families had their breadwinner or some male member interned in the Curragh by the Fianna Fail Government under the stewardship of Eamon de Valera.

The conditioning of the turbulent late twenties and early

thirties probably helped such members of the Gardai as O'Donnell to overcome the period of executions during the 'Emergency' (World War Two) as members of the Gardai. Together with fellow Garda and fellow Kerry footballer Paul Russell, Tim was one of those targeted by Eoin O'Duffy to play with Dublin and Monaghan. As Garda Commissioner, Monaghan man O'Duffy had successfully packed the Dublin hurling team of 1926 with Gardai and Army personnel and duly won the All Ireland. He was obsessed with having the same success with the Dublin footballers and compelled Russell to play with Dublin and afterwards transferred the young star to Monaghan in 1927 and 1928. O'Donnell safely weathered that storm but the dilemma which followed during the Blueshirt thirties and the IRA campaign of the forties made the playing of Gaelic football for both Republicans and Gardai a most traumatic experience at times.

O'Donnell explained the sadness and resentment rampant in the Force in those years of World War Two, especially amongst Kerry-born Gardai, when both Kerins and fellow Kerryman, Maurice O'Neill of Cahirciveen were executed. O'Neill was convicted of shooting Detective Mordaunt during a shoot-out in Donnycarney, Dublin on October 19th, 1942. The Kerry man was arrested, tried before a Military Tribunal and his sentence of death was endorsed by the Government on November 10th, 1942. Two days later Maurice O'Neill was executed by firing squad in Mountjoy. Most Kerry people were sickened by this action as it was by no means certain that O'Neill had fired the shot which killed the detective. A whole company of the LDF (FCA) Reserve Army handed in their uniforms in Waterville, near Cahirciveen.

Then, when an English hangman, Pierpoint, was brought over two years later and Tralee man Charlie Kerins was executed for the shooting of Detective O'Brien, feelings in Kerry ran dangerously high. Again, it was generally accepted that Kerins had not fired the fatal shot, though he may have given the order for the shooting. The British executioner was commissioned to hang a young Kerry man and the deed was carried out on December 1st, 1944.

When I interviewed the two sisters of Charlie Kerins, Elsie and Lena, in 1997 the sadness and impact of their loss, and the experience of their brother's trial and hanging, had obviously never subsided.

Elsie explained the trauma of being present for his two trials before Military Tribunals in the months of October and November 1944.

"I was pregnant and gave birth to my son, Cathal, on January 27th, two days after what would have been Charlie's 25th birthday," said Mrs Elsie Kerins O'Connor. [17]

She had visited her brother every day and still recalls the last words he uttered to her and her father, Thomas, on the day prior to his execution. "He was very brave. He kept all of us going during those last three weeks. There was a custom of a condemned prisoner having three Sundays to live after sentence. We made good use of those precious three weeks." [18]

Charlie's last words to his sister were: "I'm proud to die for my country and my beliefs. Very few people get the opportunity to die for their country." [19]

On the following morning at 8 o'clock the 25 year old Tralee man was hanged. After saying goodbye to his father and sisters on the previous evening at 10 p.m. he spent his final hours as follows:

10. p.m. to 3 a.m slept.

3 a.m. to 7 a.m. reading last letter to Dr. K Farrell.

7 a.m. shaved. Heard two masses and received Holy Communion.

8 a.m Hanged by English hangman, Pierpoint. [20]

Kerins had won a Kerry County Senior football Championship medal with O'Rahilly's in 1939. Five years later he was executed by the English hangman, Pierpoint.

Elsie described how her brother kept his cool demeanour even when sentenced, although his warder, fellow Kerryman, Mike Scannell from Lixnaw broke down when he heard the sentence of death by hanging passed by the court.

"December 1st, the day of the execution, was a cold harsh day"[21] and Elsie explained how she felt some grain of consolation when she thought how tough it would have been for Charlie had he been sent to the then exceptionally harsh Portlaoise Prison for life.

Mountjoy Prison Governor, Sean Kavanagh, said Kerins was the bravest man he ever saw going to the gallows. Kavanagh had watched Kerins pack his case with his personal belongings for his family in his cell before walking to his death a few minutes later. The experience was related by Kavanagh.

"OF THE PEOPLE I WAS DESTINED TO SEE DIE, THERE WAS ONE ESPECIALLY WHOSE MEMORY HAUNTS ME. HIS NAME WAS CHARLIE KERINS, CHIEF OF STAFF OF THE IRA. HE WAS THE BRAVEST MAN I EVER SAW DIE BY HANGING, ONLY 25 YEARS OF AGE, HE WAS A VERY ATTRACTIVE YOUNG MAN. I GREW TO KNOW AND LIKE HIM VERY WELL. I HAD FREQUENT DAILY MEETINGS WITH HIM BEFORE THE FATAL MORNING. AT NO TIME AFTER HIS TRIAL DID HE ENTERTAIN ANY HOPES OF A REPRIEVE, AND WHEN A FEW DAYS BEFORE HIS EXECUTION I HAD TO BRING THE NEWS THAT THE LAW MUST TAKE ITS COURSE, HE TOOK IT QUITE CALMLY AND REMARKED THAT HE HAD NEVER EXPECTED ANYTHING ELSE. UP TO THE END HE REMAINED COMPOSED, EVEN RELAXED AND COULD EVEN JOKE ABOUT HIS EXECUTION... THE EVENING BEFORE HIS DEATH HE ASKED ME IF I HAD PIECE OF ADVICE TO GIVE ABOUT THE MORNING. I SAID THAT HE NEEDED NO ADVICE FROM ME, ONLY TO SUBMIT COMPLETELY AND OFFER NO RESISTANCE. I ADDED: "LEAVE OFF YOUR TIE IN THE MORNING AND UNBUTTON YOUR COLLAR." I SAW WHEN I VISITED HIM IN THE CONDEMNED CELL BEFORE MASS NEXT MORNING THAT HE HAD LEFT OFF HIS TIE BUT THE SHIRT WAS STILL BUTTONED..... AT A MINUTE OR TWO BEFORE EIGHT O'CLOCK WHEN THE MASS HAD ENDED, I SAW FROM MY POSITION KNEELING BEHIND HIM, HIS LEFT HAND GO UP AND UNBUTTON HIS COLLAR. I MARVELLED AT HIS PRESENCE OF MIND TO REMEMBER THAT LITTLE DETAIL...THE PREVIOUS EVENING HE GAVE ME A PHOTOGRAPH OF HIMSELF SIGNED WITH "FOND REMEMBRANCE"..... BEFORE THE LAST MASS OF HIS LIFE HE ASKED TO SEE THE PHOTOGRAPH, AND CHECKING THE INSCRIPTION SAID "THAT'S ALRIGHT; I WAS THINKING DURING THE NIGHT THAT I HAD SPELLED REMEMBRANCE WRONG." [22]

Kavanagh goes on to say that much as he objected to the killing of Detective O'Brien, he admired Charlie Kerins for his courage and idealism, and never more than for the moments before his death when he stood at attention on the scaffold and submitted himself to the hands of the British executioner.

Charlie Kerins was buried within the prison walls beside his comrade and fellow Kerry man Maurice O'Neill from Cahirciveen, who had been executed by an army firing squad in November 1942. In 1948 Charlie's remains were exhumed and given to his relatives. He is now buried in Rath cemetery in his own home town of Tralee.

Tim O'Donnell described his feelings as a Garda at the time.

"I felt like leaving the Gardai when the two Kerry men, Kerins and O'Neill were executed. Feelings were running very high amongst the Kerry Gardai throughout the country. Many Kerry guards felt the same as I did. Everybody knew they were innocent but they refused to recognise the court and were executed. The father of Charlie Kerins, Tom, was active with the Strand Street Club for a time and Charlie himself had won a County Senior Championship medal Strand Street (O'Rahilly's) Tralee club in 1939." [23]

Such were the feelings in Tralee that the then O'Rahilly's club was to be renamed Kerins' O'Rahilly's after Charlie Kerins, and Tim O'Donnell's dilemma can be understood when one realises he had played with that club as a star defender in the thirties.

Tralee Austin Stack's Club member and former player, Joe Sugrue, later to be well known on the racecourses and greyhound tracks as a bookmaker, was a Dublin-based Garda when Kerins was executed in 1944. Joe resigned his job in the Gardai when the Tralee man was hanged. Kerry midfield star Paddy Kennedy eventually changed career as a result of these tragic times, as did Bill Carlos of Roscommon. Charlie O'Sullivan of Kerry was reluctant to participate in the arrest of Kerins and his opportunities for promotion were seriously affected. Winner of four All Ireland medals, Charlie O'Sullivan, was a well known figure on traffic duty at O'Connell Bridge for decades. Bill Carlos, winner of two medals in '43 and '44 with Roscommon, eventually resigned the Gardai and emigrated to the USA where he died in 1997.

Kerins was buried in Mountjoy Prison but the impact of the funeral in Kerry as an empty coffin was carried in silent procession through the town of Tralee left a deep impression on many of the thousands who lined the streets and marched. Sean Quilter, son of a former Civil War internee and Kilkenny Jail escapee, John F Quilter, who was a supporter of Fianna Fail, and a neighbour of Charlie Kerins, describes the sad night in question. Then a ten year old, he remembers: "the eerie silence as thousands of feet moved in procession. No words were spoken and only the gentle stepping and shuffling of feet was barely audible.[24] "The pressure on Fianna Fail families in Tralee and especially in Strand Road was almost unbearable. My mother told me recently that it was a very traumatic time for my father, Joe Barrett, as a supporter of Fianna Fail and De Valera, and also living in the Strand Road area, and, of course, with strong football connections.

Tim O'Donnell was born in the scenically beautiful Gleann na nGealt valley above the village of Camp on the Dingle Peninsula in 1907. His older brother, John, was eventually to become well known as the New York GAA promoter and stormy petrel of GAA affairs, John 'Kerry' O'Donnell.

An abiding love for Gaelic football was nurtured by their father and the young O'Donnell brothers figured prominently in the Camp team in West Kerry football championships.

Tim worked on the mountainous farm as a teenager while searching for a hard-to-find job and while trying to avoid the emigrant ship in which his brother, John Kerry, had gone to New York in the early twenties. Tim explained: "My father was a great follower of the game. We heard a lot about Kerry teams when we were young. I could sing off the 1914 Kerry team when I was going to school."[25]

In early 1925 the 17 year old O'Donnell travelled in the

'Ghost Train' with his father to the long-awaited 1924 All Ireland Final in which Kerry beat Dublin by 0-4 to 0-3.

The appropriately named 'Ghost Train' left Tralee at midnight on the Saturday night before the All Ireland Final. As can be imagined, the condition of some of its passengers leaving the many stations in Kerry after an evening in the pub produced a jolly pilgrimage to the capital city. The six or sometimes seven hour journey was a considerable test of endurance, character and certainly one's abiding love for football. Personally, the author witnessed a row on possibly the last ghost train, for the 1960 All Ireland Final between Kerry and Down. It began between Farranfore and Killarney, and didn't finish until Mallow. Afterwards, some slept peacefully until we arrived in Dublin.

That unheated carriage from Tralee to Dublin left an enduring memory for the young O'Donnell, but his first time in Croke Park was a memorable occasion for the West Kerry teenager who saw his county win their sixth championship Final. The thrill of seeing Kerry win the All Ireland further increased O'Donnell's appetite for personal football glory and it kindled his yearning to wear a Kerry jersey as soon as possible. "We deprived Dublin of four in a row that day, as they had won the All Ireland in 1921, 22 and 1923. Kerry had also done it in 1909, as Dublin had won in 1906, 07 and 08." [26]

Brought up on the side of the scenically hilly Dingle Peninsula, O'Donnell's athleticism blossomed and he was to become an accomplished high jumper, hop step and jumper and to cultivate his prowess at Gaelic football.

When interviewed by the author at age eighty eight he was fit and well, although an old football injury to a knee, in the All Ireland Semi-Final of 1931 against Mayo in Tuam, is a constant reminder of the legacy which most footballers carry to the grave. He admitted that his rearing and his father's enthusiasm for the game was a large contributory factor to his eventual natural strength and fitness: "I would run up the hills for the sheep instead of bringing the sheep dog. I had a mighty leap for a ball and I was lucky to have very good hands too." [27]

Kerry won a good All Ireland with a very strong team when beating Kildare in the 1926 replayed Final. But in the following two years the lifeblood of the team was seriously drained when star players Jerry Pluggy Moriarty, Patcheen Clifford, Bill Landers and Mossy Galvin emigrated to the USA. Johnny Murphy had died of meningitis between the drawn game and the replay of the 1926 decider. That they reached the Final in 1927 was a major achievement. Soon afterwards Gal Slattery, Tommy Mahony and Phil O'Sullivan were also to cross the Atlantic to further exacerbate the haemorrhage of Kerry football talent to the United States.

It was that exodus which allowed space for players like Purty Landers, Joe O'Sullivan, Pedlar Sweeney, Miko Doyle and Tim O'Donnell to make their mark with the Kingdom. O'Donnell played for Kerry in 1927 at the age of twenty, but it was two years later before he won his first All Ireland medal amongst some of the greatest players in the history of the game. A number of the older players had collected All Ireland medals in 1924 and '26 and Bob Stack, Jack Walsh from Craughdarrig (not to be confused with Johnny), Con Brosnan, Paul Russell, Jackie Ryan and team captain, Joe Barrett were to go on to collect a total of six All Irelands in all when they completed the four-in-a-row in 1932 .

Being non-political though intensely nationalistic, O'Donnell can look back at the political climate of the twenties with a neutral retrospective and his account of the interaction between the politically opposed footballers and officials of Kerry football in the twenties and thirties is worth recalling.

"There was certainly great tension in the dressing room at times when the political climate would over-boil. But, many of us would ignore the bad feelings in the air and get on with playing the game for our county. It could be very embarrassing if somebody brought up politics in the conversation. However, though I was a Garda during some bad times, I never felt any needle against me from my team mates. We were all very close." [28] They were bound to be close due to the training regime they enjoyed as Kerry players. For, even in O'Donnell's first All Ireland winning year of 1929, the Kerry team spent three weeks in full-time training in Tralee under trainer Jack McCarthy, eventual Secretary of the Munster Council of the GAA.

"We were staying in the Central Hotel in Tralee. We trained under Jack at the Sportsfield from 11 a.m until 1 o'clock when we broke for a good cooked meat lunch. It was back to training again from 3 o'clock until 5 o'clock when we went back to the hotel again for another substantial meal. After our dinner we went for a seven mile march before retiring to bed at 11 p.m.

We were very fit and the comradeship was outstanding. We would die for each other, though there were people there who were strongly opposed politically. We always broke up the training camp on Wednesday to go home for a few days. We would all meet at the 2 p.m. train for Dublin on Saturday when there was a separate carriage supplied for the team and officials. We were very well looked after and it paid off handsomely for Kerry football." [29]

Tim joined the Gardai in 1931 and his first station was at Knocknagree in County Cork where he got into trouble with the GAA for innocently breaking the Parish Rule by playing illegally. Knocknagree was in the Kerry Diocese but Tim had been misled about the rule and found himself in breach of the regulations. He was suspended, but because of his playing reputation he was immediately reinstated. He transferred to Killarney Garda area, where he played with Dr. Crokes, at the instigation of "Small" Ger O'Leary and such was Ger's influence that Timmo was transferred by the authorities by wire instead of by the statutory Form D10.

During the Kerry 'Stand down' in 1935, three Dublin based Kerry players, O'Donnell, Paddy Whitty and Paul Russell, all lined out for Dublin in the Leinster Championship.

On that team was the famous Bobby Beggs, and Timmo

recalls how the Dublin side was beaten by a mere point by Louth. O'Donnell was also a member of the Garda team which beat O'Toole's in a Dublin League Final on a day when Tim put two goals past the legendary Johnny McDonnell. "He was the best goalkeeper I ever saw, the best 'keeper ever," said the Kerry man.

Timmo celebrated his ninetieth birthday in 1997 and I had the pleasure of attending the Crofton Hotel function in Dublin when two hundred people honoured the former Kerry football star and undoubted gentleman of Gaelic football history.

Chapter 10

Con Brosnan

Of Con Brosnan, the great John Joe 'Purty Landers' said: "Con Brosnan was the political Bridge Builder of our time. And remember it wasn't always popular to try breaking moulds in those days. But Con had incredible guts and, regardless of pressure from within his own side of the divide, or from our side, he did what he believed had to be done to bring about peace and healing. He was the ultimate peacemaker in Kerry football after the Civil War." [30]

Con Brosnan gave a lifetime to the GAA in many capacities, as successful Kerry player, captain and trainer. He loved his country and the game of Gaelic football. He won six All Ireland medals in his own career and his son Jim, now a doctor in Dingle, was one of the most effective forwards in Kerry football of the 1950s, winning two All Irelands, '53 and '55. Jim also served as Kerry County Board Chairman and trainer of Kerry teams in the 1960s. Another son, Mick, was in the panel in the 1953 All Ireland win against Armagh.

Revered in North Kerry after the War of Independence and eventually the Civil War, Con Brosnan was above reproach in his credentials as a leader of men, and as one who had laid his own life on the line in the fight for freedom from Britain.

On January 19th, 1921 on the Big Fair Day, in Listowel, Con Brosnan and another Moyvane man, Jack Aherne, had confronted and shot dead District Inspector O'Sullivan of the Royal Irish Constabulary, only fifty yards from the well fortified Listowel RIC Barracks and 300 yards from the British Army Garrison. [31]

District Inspector O'Sullivan had been promoted to Listowel after, on May 28th, 1920, bravely defending Kilmallock RIC Barracks against attack from some of the most lethal IRA units from the South Tipperary Brigade, the East Limerick Brigade and the East Clare Brigade. The East Limerick Brigade Vice O.C., Tomas O Maoileoin (also known as Sean Forde), listed Dan Breen, Sean Treacy, Mick Sheehan, Mike Brennan and Sean Carroll amongst the raiding party. [32] There were some Cork and Kerry Volunteers also in the sixty strong IRA attacking force but the one to fall on that occasion was a young Kerry school teacher, Captain Liam Scully of Glencar.

He had been teaching in Strand Road National School, Tralee, a stone's throw from where Charlie Kerins was born in 1918. Scully had been shot dead as an open target from inside the RIC Barracks and the two RIC Sergeants, one of them O'Sullivan, were regarded as responsible. There was a garrison of twenty two constables accompanying O'Sullivan and he was credited with saving the lives of the seven survivors. The rest were reported to have been either burned in the blazing barracks or shot in the battle. It was generally accepted in Kerry that D.I. O'Sullivan was shot in Listowel as a reprisal for Scully's killing in Kilmallock. [33] However, O Maoileoin's account of this incident gave a much different reason for O'Sullivan's death. O Maoileoin believed it was as a result of an interception by Liam Lynch's command of an order to bring O'Sullivan to Spike Island Prison to identify the then incarcerated O Maoileoin as Sean Forde. It would have meant certain execution for O Maoileoin (Forde) as he was wanted for a string of attacks on the occupying forces. And so, accordingly, two crack IRA men, Volunteer Matt Ryan and another were sent to Listowel to shoot D.I. Tobias O'Sullivan [34]. O'Maoileoin's account could be correct up to the actual reason for the killing of O'Sullivan, but he was totally incorrect in thinking Ryan carried out the action. Con Brosnan, Jack Aherne and Danny O'Grady were the trio who killed D.I. O'Sullivan, in Listowel, and not in Moyvane as stated by O Maoileoin. Liam Scully's death had been avenged one way or the other. [35]

As a reprisal for the killing of D.I. O'Sullivan, the village of Moyvane was ransacked and Con Brosnan's home was burned to the ground by the Black and Tans.

Con Brosnan became a household name in Kerry's fighting story. He was one who had been tested and not found wanting in the heat of battle, either on or off the pitch. Brosnan became a Captain in the Free State Army during the Civil War, as an ardent supporter of Michael Collins. Of course, he and his eventual life long friend, Joe Barrett, fought on the opposite sides during that bloody Civil War in Kerry. Captain Brosnan would later put his political activity behind him in the ensuing years as he pursued a glittering career as one of Kerry's greatest ever midfielders., going on to win six All Ireland Senior medals from 1924 to 1932.

The period after the Civil War was the most crucial to the future of Kerry football as the county had not played in Croke Park for nine years and in fact had not won an All Ireland title since 1914. It is remarkable therefore what was achieved by this band of political opposites in those years after the terrible conflict. When Kerry collected their sixth All Ireland title, the '24 crown, in April 1925 it had been eleven years since they had tasted success.

Brosnan played with Kerry in the losing 1923 All Ireland Final, which was actually played on September 28th, 1924. Dublin won that clash but Kerry were to halt the four-in-a-row effort by Dublin in the 1924 championship played in April 1925. Brosnan kicked the winning point from a free in an exceptionally low scoring 0-4 to 0-3 Final.

Carbery's glowing tribute to Con Brosnan in the 1947 Annual is worth recapturing for the current reader:

"CON BROSNAN OF NORTH KERRY, RECKONED BY MANY CRITICS AS THE BEST CENTRE-FIELD MAN THAT EVER PLAYED, WAS THE MAN WHOSE PARTNERSHIP WITH BOB STACK OF BALLYBUNION MADE FOOTBALL HISTORY. THEY WERE THE IDEAL BLEND AND THEIR DOMINANCE AT MIDFIELD KEPT KERRY IN THE LIMELIGHT FROM 1922 TO 1932 AND BEYOND, WINNING SIX ALL IRELANDS-THE LAST FOUR, 1929 - 1932 IN A ROW TO EQUAL WEXFORD'S RECORD. CON BROSNAN WAS A STRONG, HANDSOME, 5-10 MAN, 12 STONE, BEAUTIFULLY MOULDED. LIKE BOB STACK, "HE COULD HOLD GOING ALL DAY." CON WAS A

POLISHED FOOTBALLER, GRAND FIELDER, CLEVER ANTICIPATION, KICKS PER-
FECTLY PLACED. HE COULD "LACE" HOME A POINT FROM 50 YARDS ON
DEMAND, DROP KICK, BREAK, PASS CLEVERLY, RACE THROUGH IN LONG SOLO
RUNS, FAST RISING GROUND SHOTS FOR GOALS OR POINTS, GRAND FEEDER OF
FORWARDS, HE REMINDED ME AT TIMES OF ANOTHER CON - THE GREAT
KILLARNEY MAN - CONNIE MURPHY. CON BROSNAN PLAYED A MAN'S PART
IN OUR NATIONAL STRUGGLE. HE SUFFERED MUCH AND HIS HEALTH SUF-
FERED." [36]

To show the extent of his popularity in the county, a poem
was written in tribute to Con Brosnan, who went on to win six
All Ireland medals.

"The All Ireland Final 1924"

"The 26th we shall long remember
As the sun's bright rays down the hilltop rolled
And shone in beauty where the teams did duty,
The boys in blue and in green and gold.

The brilliant bands in that grand arena,
Announced the coming of a struggle rare,
Whilst seas of faces filled all the spaces
And for once old Ireland seemed free from care.

Full 30,000 were anxious waiting
The Triple Champions again to see,
The coin was spun the Kingdom won
And the teams were slipped by the referee.

Bob Stack for Kerry secured the leather,
His mighty drive against wind and sun,
Put the blues defending their lines were bending,
Their fort was stormed by the Kingdom's gun.

And at centrefield where the fight was raging,
Shone Brosnan bright as the morning star,

He drove the leather right up to Landers,
Who fisted neatly across the bar.
Now Dublin hard for a goal were trying,
But their forward flying received a shock,
He bounded onward in deerlike fashion
But came to grief on the Kerry rock.

For a rock he is the famed Joe Barrett,
With Phil the peerless the true and tried,
And Johnnie Murphy in the ruck shone brightly,
Those three defenders all foes denied.

And who could venture past Jack Walsh at centre,
He was never once through the hour at fault,
And fast and clever in each endeavour,
Moriarty ever to a rush cried halt.

In a mighty tussle we saw Paul Russell,
From a sea of jerseys the leather steal,
The hearts of Kerry sprang forth to greet him,
Their cheers re-echoed along the Feale.

And Ryan and Sheehy combining neatly,
And "Mundy" always outshining Joe,
The tide of battle was at its highest
And we were watching its ebb and flow.

But the Dublin team were far from yielding
As they tried to do as they did before
But Sheehy great from the net appearing
Beat back the raiders without a score.

The scene now changed to the Dublin Fortress,
The players encouraged by the Kingdom's roar,
And the brothers Baily swept all before them
To try beat McDonnell for the major score.

But once again we were disappointed,
The score denied us and the end drawing near,
But a silver lining through a dark cloud shining,
A glorious moment we saw appear.

'Twas a free to Kerry,
Con Brosnan took it,
With steady nerve and unerring aim,
He scored a point and again we led them
'Twas the final flag in a hard fought game.

Hats off to Brosnan that midfield wonder,
He's par excellence with feet and hands,
Where is the Gael can bring down the number
Of Kerry's idol from Newtownsandes."[37]

The reconciliation which had gone into the rebuilding of Kerry's football fabric in the preceding year, since the jails and internment camps had opened, is one for which Con Brosnan can take much of the credit, according to many of his peers from all sides of the political divisions over the decades.

This resetting of Kerry's footballing foundation stone after eleven barren years was to produce a run of success which saw the Kingdom gain eleven All Ireland Senior football titles from 1924 to 1941, a total of 18 years. In the two decades of Ireland's most turbulent political climate, Kerry went on a feeding frenzy which produced an All Ireland win, on average, almost every second year. And this was achieved against a background of immense political tension, in the face, many times, of overheated political passions which called for great effort in healing and patience.

According to those contemporaries of Con Brosnan, who still survive, he was the one who tolerated no political discussion in football dressing rooms or gatherings where football was the main concern. Johnny Walsh of Ballylongford who was another but younger contemporary of Con Brosnan recalled a trip to Dublin by train when Walsh as an enthusiastic supporter of Brosnan, the youngster preferred some unsolicited comment on the current political question.

Walsh told the author: "Con shut me up by saying, don't ever speak politics again on a football train." [38]

Con Brosnan was born on St. Stephen's Day 1900 and educated in Listowel. He was son of the local Creamery Manager in the north Kerry village of Newtownsandes, later changed to its present name of Moyvane under the instigation of community leader Brosnan. The name of Sandes represented the Anglo Saxon landlord ruling class and was not acceptable to the nationalistic Brosnan, thus the change of name to Moyvane.

By the time the War of Independence began, Con Brosnan was deeply involved and became a member of the Derry IRA Unit attached to the North Kerry Flying Column. It was this Unit which entered Listowel to shoot District Inspector O'Sullivan dead in 1921.

Together with the shooting dead of Head Constable Benson by Tommy Driscoll of Kilmoyley, Ardfert, in Pembroke Street, Tralee, this was one of the severest blows and flagrant affronts suffered by the rule of the RIC in North Kerry during the War of Independence.

As a former IRA hero, Brosnan was a highly respected Kerry Free State Officer in the eyes of HQ during the Civil War. Although strong Republican, Dan Bally Keating would tell the author in 1997: "Brosnan was never a real Free Stater." And when Con Brosnan was an organiser in Kerry for the Army Comrades Association, the ACA (The Blueshirt movement), he resigned the position in a storm of publicity.

If Brosnan's record as a freedom fighter is worthy of note, then his contribution to Kerry football as a player, administrator and reconciliator is monumental.

However, when Brosnan was initially tasting the thrills of inter-county football, the turmoil of the political scene prevented fully representative wearing of the green and gold jersey.

The prisons, hills and dugouts contained many eligible Kerry footballers, as men on the run and incarcerated deprived Kerry of their best team. From when they contested the 1920 Munster Final, losing to Tipperary on April 9th, 1922 until the 1923 All Ireland Final which they lost to Dublin, Kerry football was paralysed by the Troubles. There had been no Munster Championship in 1921 and, due to the ravages of the Civil War in March 1923 in Kerry, they withdrew from a fixture against Limerick.

The 1923 Munster Final played on October 14th, '23, was won by Kerry with a stranger, a Dubliner named Bermingham, who was a Free State soldier, on the side. Con Brosnan was absent from that team, though he played in the strengthened team which lost to Dublin in the postponed All Ireland Final played on September 28th, 1924. The Internment Camps were open and Kerry was about to launch on its rebuilding of Gaelic games within the county.

Brosnan had led the Kerry team to play the Ex-Internees in two games, which exposed the combined football talent of the pro and anti-treaty sides in Kerry. It was to bring together also the people who followed differing political ideals. Players like Con Brosnan and John Joe Sheehy, who were what Con Casey referred to as "deadly enemies", now became football friends."

On the occasion of the Munster Final in Limerick between Kerry and Clare in 1924, when John Joe Sheehy was still on the run, it fell to Con Brosnan to get a guarantee of safe passage from the authorities for the Kerry forward. This enabled the star forward to play in the game and then vanish into the countryside without arrest.

The sensitive line these men walked is evidenced in the words of Con Casey when he described the funeral of his brother-in-law, Charlie Daly, who was executed during the Civil War in Drumboe Castle, Co. Donegal on March 14th, 1923 by the Free State Army.

"When we brought Charlie home for burial in 1926 it was Con Brosnan who was in charge of the large Free State Army contingent at the very tense funeral at which John Joe Sheehy was the key IRA leader of the Guard of Honour and chief organiser of the tense funeral ceremony." [39]

When in 1996 at the age of 97, Con Casey was asked by the author, just how Brosnan and Sheehy tolerated each other over such a long time associated as players and selectors with Kerry teams, he replied:

"They had a mutual respect for each other and kept away from each other unless it was totally unavoidable." [40]

The relationship between Brosnan and Sheehy had been an uneasy one between two very strong characters and powerful personalities. The conflict of opposites theory was tested to its fullest and certainly produced undoubted progress for the good of Gaelic football. Many sacrifices had been made and animosities laid tentatively to rest. And all of this was achieved "in the name of the game."

Chapter 11

Joe Barrett

For most people it is difficult to talk about one's own family and remain objective. I am no exception. Compounding the task further is the fact that my father died when I was nine. So while my memories are clear, they are boyish impressions and I never knew him through the eyes of an adult. Therefore, apart from my mother's recollections, this profile is constructed from the opinions and impressions of him from people who knew him well.

He carried his love for Gaelic football to the grave but left a legacy of this love for Gaelic games to his family. His son, Tim, captained the Kerry Minor team in the 1954 All Ireland Final which Kerry lost to Dublin. Tim shared a record with the great Jackie Lyne of Killarney (uncle of the Spillane brothers) for having been selected on three consecutive Munster Colleges Teams. He also played senior for Kerry before emigrating to England at 19 years of age, thus ending any hope of fulfilling his true football potential. Joe's eldest son, John, won two Munster Colleges medals with Tralee CBS on the same team as Tim and also played minor hurling and junior football for Kerry. John became a prominent sports journalist with The Kerryman, Irish Press and Irish Post in London. Tim died in 1973 and John died in 1995. Both held strong Republican views throughout their lives.

I never had the opportunity to have political discussions with my father, but I have vivid memories of his absolute admiration for De Valera. I had the opportunity to meet De Valera as a young election worker for Fianna Fail. Dev and Fianna Fail received exceptionally strong support in Tralee but the political divisions in the Kerry capital affected most of the population. The situation was exacerbated by the executions of Kerry republicans. However, I didn't live through those times and I would not envy my father his dilemma as a Republican during that period.

Joe Barrett was born on July 17th, 1902, into a nationalistic family home at 67 Rock Street, Tralee, the house in which he was to draw his last breath on June 2nd, 1952. He was the third of five sons and six daughters to Tralee pig and cattle dealer, John Barrett. His mother, Nora O'Mahony, was from the North Kerry parish of Ballyduff.

In his relatively short life he took part in the War of Independence as a Volunteer and was to take an active part in the Civil War until his arrest and incarceration. Dan Bally Keating describes a night on which Barrett and others from the Rock Street column, including Christy Ryan, Bobby Rucky Kelly, Johnny Roche and Joe Sugrue, disarmed six Black and Tans at the old Dingle railway station and made a safe getaway with the precious weapons and ammunition.[41] However, his greatest mark on life would be left in the form of a brilliant football career in which he became a national sports hero as a great full-back and as a man of distinct leadership qualities as a successful team captain.

The influence in his home was strongly Catholic and nationalist. As a teenager he would also have been influenced by the resistance in Tralee to the dying kick of the Kerry Unionists. When the Volunteers were formed in 1914 Joe's eldest brother, Christy, was one of the founding members of the Tralee movement. When Pearse spoke in Tralee in February 1916 my father was among the youngsters who admired this stranger from the great and distant city of Dublin. Pearse's real legacy was to be left two months later.

The only notable account of Joe Barrett's teenage years was gathered from a local newspaper account of his being fined for playing handball against a Jim O'Connor's wall with an eventual fellow Republican Robert Kelly, a neighbour. They were twelve years old. Coincidentally, the same two were to be involved in the incident with the Black and Tans, as mentioned above.

The patriot Thomas Ashe from West Kerry, who died on hunger strike, was a regular guest in the Barrett house during Barrett's impressionable years and the house was used for the concealing of some of the meagre weapon supply which the Volunteers had in their possession.

1916 was a bad year for Kerry, as the leading Republican Austin Stack shouldered much blame after the failure of the Roger Casement landing on Banna Strand. Monteith wrote: "Casement was cast ashore on his native land without a word of welcome, no hand outstretched to help him, outlawed, a price upon his head."[42] To this day the Easter Week fiasco in Banna can raise much debate but the simple practical problems of communications of the time were a definite contributory factor for the mixup. I always felt pity for Stack who was directed to the wrong part of Banna beach looking for Casement. Banna Beach is ten miles long with deep sand hills. There are various place names along the foreshore, which in Tralee were all referred to as Banna in those less informed times of little communication. When Casement was eventually arrested it was at Currahane/Brandonwell, which is wedged in between Banna, Ardfert, Knockenaugh and Barrow. Only a local would know the names in 1916, and Austin Stack was a Tralee man from eight miles away. Casement was a total stranger to the area.

In his book, Casement's Last Adventure, Captain Robert Monteith, who had come ashore in Tralee Bay with Sir Roger Casement from the German submarine on the morning of April 21st, 1916, explained the various misunderstandings which led to Casement's arrest and eventual execution by hanging in Pentonville Prison in England.

Casement's suffering was indeed great, being subjected to the ignominy of execution by the common English hangman, John Ellis, who also hanged such notorious murderers as Dr. Crippen and Edith Thompson.[43] Monteith wondered would it have been better that the April moonlit waves of Banna Strand had claimed the patriot's life instead.

"HAD I KNOWN THE ENDING OF THE CHAPTER I WOULD SURELY HAVE LET HIM SLIP INTO ETERNITY IN THE FOAMING WATER ON BANNA STRAND, THE WATER THAT HAD TRIED TO BE KIND TO ONE OF IRELAND'S HEROES." [44]

Of his experience, after eventually finding his way to Tralee and making contact with Tralee Volunteer Commander, Austin Stack, Monteith wrote:

"I THEN ASKED STACK ABOUT THE NON-APPEARANCE OF THE PILOT BOAT. HE GAVE TO UNDERSTAND THAT AS FAR AS HIS INSTRUCTIONS WENT, THE SHIP (AUD) WAS NOT DUE UNTIL SUNDAY NIGHT. WHEN WORD CAME THAT THE CAR WAS READY I DIRECTED BEVERLEY (BAILEY) TO GO WITH IT AS GUIDE TO CASEMENT'S HIDING PLACE. THEY LEFT ME TO GO TO SIR ROGER; MISS SPICER ACCOMPANIED THEM IN ORDER TO GIVE IT THE APPEARANCE OF A PLEASURE TRIP. I SAW STACK, COLLINS AND BEVERLEY (BAILEY) NO MORE. THAT NIGHT I HEARD THAT STACK AND COLLINS WERE ARRESTED BUT THAT BEVERLEY (BAILEY) HAD ESCAPED. THESE TWO MEN WERE TRIED AND SEN- TENCED TO IMPRISONMENT FOR LIFE. BEVERLEY (BAILEY) WAS LATER ARREST- ED AND TRIED IN LONDON, BUT ACQUITTED." [45]

Whatever about the whys and wherefores of the Casement fiasco, 1916 was also the year Joe Barrett followed his older brother Christy into the family pig and cattle business. After their father John Barrett died at age 57 in 1915, Christy was head of the family which included six sisters and five brothers. World War One was at its fiercest and the export of bacon and other meats created a huge demand which kept the Barretts gainfully employed through their agency for the two local bacon factories, CWS and Slatterys (now Dennys), and for some Cork and Limerick bacon factories. At fourteen, Joe was now fully involved, learning the business which he had been raised to anyway. Droving, feeding and cleaning out from ani- mals was usually the chore of the younger male members of the household in those days.

Tragedy was to again strike the family two years later when the eldest brother, Christy, died on November 15th, 1918, at age

30, after contracting pneumonia during the great 'flu epidemic. Christy, while recovering from flu, had crossed the Shannon to a cattle fair in County Clare by open boat and the resultant wetting caused his fatal illness.

The onus fell to Joe at 16, and Jimmy 14, to hold the business together and at such a tender age it was a baptism of fire in a most competitive industry which required a great deal of credibility, honour and ready cash. In that business, a man's word in a deal, sealed with the spit and slap on a hand, was binding. Both farmer and dealer accepted this method as a bond of the trade. To buy up to six railway wagons of pigs and pay for them at a fair needed a ready bankroll and the fairs were held almost five days a week.

As a boy, I remember my Aunt, Kitty Galvin, telling me that her father and brothers had a commission of one shilling per pig when there was such heavy demand for bacon during the First World War in Europe. While it does not sound like much it was enough to sustain the large family.

There is little known about Joe Barrett's football prowess before the trouble times. Snooker and billiards were very popular in the towns of Kerry. There were at least six men's clubs in Tralee. In later years my father was County Champion on a number of occasions and once in the thirties played an exhibition with Tommy O'Brien (of classical music fame). Tommy was Irish champion.

Greyhounds were another big love of Joe's life, as open coursing kept hundreds of Tralee people busy on every Sunday morning from October to March, and the inevitable game of cards rounded off the day.

When the War of Independence began, Joe was 17. He and his younger brother Jimmy were active immediately. Later, he and Jimmy and younger brother Tommy, who was a Fianna Boy, and his two sisters Nora (Enright) and Brigid (Carrick) were active in the Civil War.

While on the run, Joe was arrested between Tralee and Abbeydorney in September 1922 and spent until December

1923 in Hare Park Internment Camp. His description of his arrest and the ignominy of being marched down Rock Street past his own mother and family to jail was an abiding memory for my father.

In his book "My Fight For Irish Freedom", the great Dan Breen recalled his feelings when similarly treated on his arrest by the Free State Army, his own fellow countrymen:

"The humiliation and agony which I endured during that short march I shall never forget. May the reader never know what it is to be marched, a prisoner, through his native town for doing what he believed to be his duty in the cause of his country." [46]

Joe Barrett's health began to decline as early as 1945. In fact, one day while walking with his wife out by Ballyard he noticed that he could not keep up with her. This for a man who walked to fairs twenty miles away and who walked from Tralee to Ballyheigue as training, indicated something serious indeed. It was followed by an experimental and most unsuccessful operation for blood pressure at the Mater Hospital in Dublin. This resulted in a stroke and some very bad years of disability before his death in June, 1952.

Around that time my mother prevailed on him to document some of his past career in football and the Troubles, to pass on to his children. Some scant scribbled notes, on his IRA activities only, by the uninterested dying man are all that survive. I personally kept them safely since I first read them in my early teens. And while growing up it is strange the significance they held for me. I suppose they were the only link for me with activities from my father's life other than from his football career.

From that Diary, in his own writing, Joe Barrett revealed joining the Volunteers before his fifteenth birthday and these extracts show he had been relatively active.

These are direct transcriptions from Joe Barrett's 1936 Diary.

"APRIL 1ST, 1917 TO MARCH 31ST, 1918 UNDER OC M DOYLE, DRILLING

AND TRAINING." (BARRETT WAS LESS THAN 15 WHEN JOINING AND LESS
THAN SIXTEEN WHEN FINISHED TRAINING).

"APRIL 1ST, 1918 TO MARCH 1919 D CO. NO ONE BATT. KERRY NO I
BRIGADE. OUR OC WAS PADDY BARRY, DRILLING AND TRAINING; JOE
SUGRUE, PADDY BARRY, MICHAEL DOYLE. "

"APRIL 1ST, 1919 TO MARCH 31ST, 1920 OC JOHN O'CONNOR. JOHN
ROCHE, RORY O'CONNELL, JOE SUGRUE."

"ASSISTED IN THE GENERAL ATTACK ON TRALEE. WAS ARMED."

"ASSISTED IN THE ATTACK ON FENIT BARRACKS. BLOCKADING ETC., AND
GUARDING CITIZENS WHO WERE THREATENED. WITH JOE SUGRUE, JOHN
ROCHE, CHRISTY RYAN."

"1920 - 1921 O.C. JOHN O'CONNOR, REQUESTED TO STAY AT HOME TO
BE IN READINESS FOR THE SHOOTING OF HEAD CONSTABLE BENSON."

"O.C. D CO JOE SUGRUE. 1921 TO 1922, RESISTING ATTACK ON TANS.
STANDING TO WITH COMPANY FOR ABOUT SIX WEEKS ARMED. JOE SUGRUE,
JOHN ROCHE, CHRISTY RYAN."

"O.C. D COMPANY JOHNNY O'SULLIVAN. 1922 TO 1923. ASSISTED IN
PREVENTING FREE STATE TROOPS LANDING IN TRALEE. ARRESTED IN
SEPTEMBER. BROUGHT TO TRALEE JAIL AND FROM THERE TO LIMERICK AND
THEN TO HARE PARK. 16 DAYS HUNGER STRIKE IN HARE PARK CAMP AND
5 DAYS IN TRALEE JAIL."

"JOE SUGRUE, RORY O'CONNELL, PADDY PAUL FITZGERALD. APRIL 1923
TO SEPTEMBER 30. RELEASED FROM HARE PARK DECEMBER 1923. O.C. TOM
HALES. ASSISTING IN MAKING TUNNELS." [47]

Joe's reference to the attack on Fenit Barracks is described in
"Kerry's Fighting Story", the attack on Fenit Barracks in June,
1920 is described:

"THE ASSAULT BEGAN AT MIDNIGHT. THE BARRACKS WAS GUTTED AND A
SHELL FROM A BRITISH GUNBOAT IN THE BAY EXPLODED HARMLESSLY ON A
NEARBY STRAND. REINFORCEMENTS FROM THE GUNBOAT COMPELLED THE
ATTACKERS TO WITHDRAW. THE BARRACKS WAS OF NO FURTHER USE." [48]

The Christy Ryan mentioned in a number of incidents with
my father was brother of Jackie Ryan who later won six All

Ireland medals with Joe. The mild mannered Christy was a familiar figure in his daily bread delivery round for Barry's Bakery, Rock Street. His eventual employer, Paddy Barry was O.C. D Company, Kerry Number I Brigade, IRA.

Kerry was not a pleasant place in which to live during those four years of conflict as a state of war prevailed in which shootings, reprisals, house burnings, curfews, and general disruption of normal life was common. For the young Barrett brothers, getting to pig and cattle fairs in places as scattered as Dingle, Kenmare, Knocknagree, Listowel, Cahirciveen, Killarney, Abbeyfeale, Castlegregory and Millstreet was a difficult task. Travel to these fairs entailed leaving home at 4 a.m.

Known Republican families were constantly harassed by the British forces and later by the Free State Army during the Civil War. Regular nocturnal raids on known active members and sympathisers was a constant danger. My aunt recalled her mother often hiding a revolver in the heavy skirts worn by the older women of those times. Tralee also suffered strictly enforced curfew after the key British figures (MacKinnon, Auxiliary, and Benson, RIC) were killed in separate incidents.

As mentioned earlier, the GAA in Kerry went through a lean period during the War of Independence and the Civil War and though there was very little organised competition for club and county teams, the memory of Kerry's fifth and last All Ireland victory in 1914 obviously kept the flame burning, if very faintly, until their next success in the 1924 All Ireland football Final, not played until 1925.

There were no County Championships played in Kerry in 1915 and '16 or for five years from 1920 to 1924, inclusive, during which many of the young men were otherwise engaged in the fight for freedom.

While little is known of the limited football activity in the few years prior to the Troubles, we know that at 17 Barrett was playing some football within his own Rock Street club. According to some contemporaries, Joe was beginning to show signs of his future ability. However, it wasn't until Barrett came out of jail in early 1924 that he had reached the standard of inter-county competition.

His brother Christy had been one of the driving forces behind the founding of the Rock Street Club in 1917 when he bought the first set of jerseys just a year before he died. The "Rock Club" (Rock Street) was to be renamed The Austin Stack's Hurling and Football Club after the great Tralee patriot who died in 1929. It was eventually known as "the street of champions" as a result of the deeds of its players in the twenties and thirties. Its record All Ireland medal collection is unequalled in the history of Gaelic football. The club once lined out fourteen Rock men on a Munster football team and Barrett was to become one of the driving forces behind its success. The total tally of senior All Ireland medals for the club, as at August 1997, stood at eighty. It has increased by two medals, as Pa Laide and Billy Kirby represented the club in the 1997 All Ireland Final in which Kerry beat Mayo.

The Barrett family circle was fortunate not to lose a single life during the Troubles but family life must have been seriously disrupted due to the imprisonment of Joe, his younger brother, Jimmy, his sister Brigid and brothers-in-law Johnny Galvin, Paddy Enright and Henry Carrick in various jails. Another sister Nora, who was active in Cumann na mBan, was arrested but escaped with a neighbour, Nora Hurley.

With the father and Christy by then dead and no male member of the family earning, the financial resources were seriously drained and so when the Curragh Internment Camp released Joe and Jimmy, plus their sister Brigid who was also interned in Kilmainham, there was a major task ahead to rebuild their by then non-existent pig and cattle buying business. When 20 year old Joe realised their release was imminent he wrote to his mother to cash their few remaining assets so as to have cash for their first "Fair Day" in Tralee Pig Market.

Little did the Barrett brothers realise what faced them when

Joe, Jimmy and their young teenage brother, Tommy, approached that fateful fair in Tralee Market on that winter's day in 1924. There were few Republican followers amongst the Tralee families who constituted the livestock buying industry in the county in the tense period of Civil War Kerry. Traditionally the pig and cattle dealing business was run by families and they were, usually, fairly comfortably off and would generally be establishment supporters.

When the Barretts entered that first fair after being released from the Internment Camps they were shunned, "as if we had the plague," my uncle Tommy Barrett told me. Indeed, the scars of such ostracisation by life-long family friends and some relatives left a hurt which took a long while to heal. However, they had anticipated this as it was not uncommon. I suppose it was understandable given the bitter Civil War that went before. Yet they knew that money talks and were prepared to pay over the odds for produce so as to re-establish themselves in the trade.

Tommy admitted years later: "Joe and Jimmy paid well over the odds at that fair to re-establish ourselves as a force in the markets of Kerry after the long lay-off."

Joe Barrett won his first of six All Ireland Senior football Championship medals in April 1925 (the '24 decider) and went on to win eight Munster Championships, Two Tailteann Games medals in which Ireland played America, National Leagues, Railway Cups and seven Kerry County football Championships, and three hurling championships. His brother Tommy won two All Ireland medals and together with Jimmy and the youngest brother Eddie, won a number of football championships with Rock Street/Austin Stack's.

Joe became a constant member of that record breaking Kerry era and duly built up a great friendship with Con Brosnan of Moyvane, who equally became a household name as midfield partner to the great Bob Stack and shared in all of this success.

In his famous captain's article from his Carbery's Annual of 1947, P D Mehigan wrote of Barrett:

"JOE BARRETT OF TRALEE STILL SPOKEN OF AS THE GREATEST FULL-BACK THAT EVER PLAYED FOR KERRY. BORN AT ROCK STREET, TRALEE, IN 1902, JOE WAS 23 WHEN HE WON HIS FIRST ALL IRELAND - HE HAD PLAYED IN THE TEAM THAT LOST TO DUBLIN IN 1923- 1-5 TO 1-3. FROM HIS EARLIEST APPEARANCE AT INTER-COUNTY HE SEEMED TO FIT IN INSTINCTIVELY TO THE VITAL FULL-BACK POSITION FOR WHICH HIS PHYSIQUE AND MENTAL EQUIP-MENT ADMIRABLY SUITED HIM. STANDING 5-10, HE RARELY SCALED LESS THAN 14 STONE AND WAS 14-7 IN HIS LATER FOOTBALL YEARS. HE HAD THE STRENGTH AND PLUCK OF A LION. HE WAS BOTH COOL AND RESOLUTE. HE TORE HIS WAY OUT OF DIFFICULTIES, HE COULD SOAR HIGH FOR A BALL, NEVER MISSED A CATCH, HIS KICKS WERE LONG AND WINGING. HE SAVED SCORES OF GOALS ON THE LINE, HE HAD BOUNDING ENERGY AND CAPTAINED MANY TEAMS AT HOME, AND AWAY - HIS BAG INCLUDES SIX ALL IRELANDS, TWO TAILTEANN INTERNATIONAL CHAMPIONSHIPS, FOUR NATIONAL LEAGUES, NINE MUNSTER CHAMPIONSHIPS, SEVEN KERRY TITLES EACH IN HURLING AND FOOTBALL. BEAUTY OF IT ALL, JOE BARRETT NEVER LOST AN HOUR AT HIS PROFESSION, THROUGH ALL HIS LONG FOOTBALL CAREER - AN IRON MAN." [49]

In Kerry the County Championship winning club has the nominating of the Kerry team captain for the following year. Rock Street, Tralee had by 1931 changed their name to honour the Republican patriot and Minister in the first Provisional Government, Austin Stack. So, after Austin Stack's won anoth-er championship in 1930, my father was again appointed Kerry skipper.

He was to test fate and no small amount of his own person-al courage when he announced that he was passing the cap-taincy over to North Kerryman, Con Brosnan, from Moyvane. To add insult to injury for the strongly Republican Rock Club, Brosnan had been a Free State Army Captain and the idea of his being presented with a Kerry captaincy by Joe Barrett was unacceptable to a great number of Rock Street people.

A determined block of opposition surfaced immediately in the three Tralee clubs, Austin Stack's, John Mitchel's and O'Rahilly's. It was felt that a Tralee player should receive the honour of captaincy if a Stack's player didn't utilise the opportunity. There was also, of course, a very extreme Republican opposition to Brosnan which was to raise its head most vociferously. This same undercurrent was never far from the surface, even in later years but was never fully activated.

Joe Barrett, with the support of John Joe (Purty) and Tim (Roundy) Landers, stuck by his decision which was to eventually get the support of his club. Republican activists and sympathisers in our club called meetings and attempted to undermine Joe Barrett's support. Brosnan accepted the Captaincy and brought the Sam Maguire to Kerry for the third consecutive year. This fairytale ending to the 1931 Captaincy issue saw Brosnan captain Kerry to beat Kildare by 1-11 to 0-8 in a hectic Final which Kildare had dominated for long periods, including most of the first half.

For years afterwards my father had to overcome a deep resentment amongst a small but strong minority in our club. Indeed, one could argue that his losing the club's nomination for the County Senior football Selection Committee, on his deathbed, was a residue from the captaincy controversy of 1931. Some believed that the lingering resentment once more surfaced as the dying Barrett was voted out at the Club's annual convention. Practically speaking, he could never have attended another match at that stage and maybe those who organised the vote against him were practical people. But when Con Brosnan heard it in North Kerry, he had Barrett co-opted as a sixth selector, and chairman of the selection committee.

On the year following the Brosnan captaincy controversy my father was again back as Kerry Captain and led the Kingdom, with two new names, Johnny Walsh and Con Geaney, on to success. This was the year he added his sixth and final All Ireland medal, as did Con Brosnan, Bob Stack, Jack Walsh, Paul Russell and Jackie Ryan. They formed this select club of six record holders until Danno Keeffe got his seventh in 1946. Of the five with six All Ireland medals: Con had been an Army Captain, Paul Russell a Civic Guard, Jackie Ryan and Joe

Barrett had been IRA, while Bob Stack and Jack Walsh would have been supporters of Con Brosnan.

They were a motley crew, holding disparate political beliefs, but on the football field fired with a united purpose. It was to nurture in Kerry the pride and brotherly love that was shattered during the Civil War. Those 36 All Ireland medals won by Ryan, Walsh, Stack, Russell, Brosnan and Barrett were more than just gold to the people of the Kingdom in post Civil War Kerry society.

Of course this record sextet lost some of their gloss in the eighties when the magical performances of the brilliant Kerry team earned Mike Sheehy, Ger Power, Pat Spillane, Ogie Moran and Paidi O Se a record eight senior medals each.

Joe Barrett was known to have a short fuse in certain circumstances. In the 1937 All Ireland Final (drawn game), as a Kerry selector he left the dugout to administer what he believed was justice. A Cavan player had seemingly been dealing out some heavy treatment to a young Kerry player, Tim O'Leary. Joe's action was totally out of order and gave my mother her first sense of the extreme side of Gaelic football. It was her first time being at a football match, and a baptism of fire. The picture of that row hung in our home for decades and shows Rock Street club players, Purty Landers, Miko Doyle and Roundy Landers, and Charlie O'Sullivan of Dingle, rushing to Joe Barrett's assistance. Who says the 'one-in-all-in' syndrome began in the nineties? In Rock Street it was always the rule.

That tight knit community spirit prevailed until recent times, when we won an All Ireland Club title in 1977. Since its formation in 1917 and its advent into senior championship in 1926, the legendary Rock Street/ Austin Stack's Club has become a historic name throughout the Gaelic football world. Through the struggle for independence and the Civil War it had produced a tradition of Republicanism. Greyhounds sports, football, hurling, Game Cock fighting, Pitch and Toss and cardgames were everyday interests for the closely bound community and a poem written by Ned Drummond, the father of a prominent Republican Rock Street family, is a suitable means by which to show the close community atmosphere that made the street so great.

> *If you want to be happy the rest of your life,*
> *Come up to the top of the Rock.*
> *It's the grandest spot in Ireland*
> *And it's full of the rare auld stock*
> *No matter what your past may be*
> *If you haven't the price of a block*
> *They'll never see you down and out*
> *Above at the top of the Rock.*
>
> *Our glorious Gaelic footballers*
> *Are champions of Tralee,*
> *They've beaten all before them*
> *From Strand Road to Boherbee,*
> *Purty plays full-forward*
> *And Barrett stands the shock*
> *You can back your bottom dollar*
> *On the boys from the top of the Rock.*
>
> *Our sporty men of different shades*
> *Their equals can't be found*
> *Lovers of the feathered race*
> *The horse, the rod and hound*
> *You have Rory O'Connell's "Fanbelt"*
> *And Paddy Casey's cock*
> *Bred, born and reared*
> *Above at the top of the Rock.* (50)

(Note: Rory O'Connell's "Fanbelt" was a greyhound and Paddy Casey was an avid Game Cock breeder, the block referred to was tobacco.)

Thinking back on those traumatic years of my father's long

illness during my childhood in Tralee, I recall most of all how my father looked forward to the visits of Con Brosnan. The Moyvane man was a regular visitor to his one-time political enemy, and remained one of his most respected friends until Joe's death. As a kid I remember being in the room on dark winter afternoons when little was said between them as Con sat patiently by Joe's sick bed, keeping him company. One sensed the history to their strong friendship. Yet at that age I did not realise how special was the bond of their past interaction. Looking back now, it is easy to see the quality of that relationship. Remember, at that stage, I had not yet seen the medals or got to know the significance of their history.

Con and Joe were special Kerrymen in a special generation of Kerry footballers. For generations of Kerry people those names from the darkest political days in recent Irish history had meant more than just football, they had also gradually eased a people away from the slavery of hatred.

The six men profiled in this book shared exactly the same Nationalistic goals but had very different beliefs in how they could be achieved. Although the colours were exactly the same, where a flag failed to unite them, a football jersey did.

Sources Chapter 6 - 11

(1) Sheehy, Brian. Interview.

(2) Harrington, Niall C. Kerry Landing. (1992) p49.

(3) Gaughan, J. Anthony. Austin Stack, Portrait of a Separatist. p286.

(4) MacEoin, Uinseann. Survivors. (1980). p357.

(5) Casey, Con. Interview.

(6) Herlihy, Jim. The Royal Irish Constabulary. 1997. pp156, 198.

(7) Harrington, Niall C. Kerry Landing. (1992) p131.

(8) Carbery's Annual 1947. pp40, 41.

(9) Walsh, Johnny. Interview.

(10) Manning, Maurice. The Blueshirts. pp107, 108. (I.T 7th., 8th, October 1933).

(11) Barry, John. and Horan Eamon. Years of Glory. (1977) p79.

(12) Landers, J .J. (Purty). Interview.

(13) Costello, Tomo. Interview.

(14) Manning, Maurice. The Blueshirts. p107.

(15) An Phoblacht. February 1934.

(16) The Earl of Longford and Thomas P O'Neill. Eamon De Valera. p302.

(17) Kerins O'Connor, Elsie. Interview.

(18) Ibid.

19) Ibid.

(20) Charlie Kerins 1944- 1994. Booklet produced by Tralee Republicans to commemorate 50th. Anniversary of death of Charlie Kerins. p18.

(21) Kerins O'Connor, Elsie. Interview.

(22) Charlie Kerins 1944-1994. Booklet p19.

(23) O'Donnell, Tim. Interview.

(24) Quilter, Sean. Interview.

(25) O'Donnell, Tim. Interview.

(26) Ibid.

(27) Ibid.

(28) Ibid.

(29) Ibid.

(30) Landers, John Joe (Purty). Interview.

(31) Keating, Dan. Interview.

(32) Mac Eoin, Uinseann. Survivors. p87 and 88.

(33) Keating, Dan. Interview.

(34) Mac Eoin, Uinseann. Survivors. p94.

(35) Brosnan, Jerry. Interview.

(36) Carbery, Famous Captains 1947.

(37) Poem Con Brosnan.

(38) Walsh, Johnny. Interview.

(39) Casey, Con. Interview.

(40) Ibid.

(41) Keating, Dan. Interview.

(42) Monteith, Captain Robert. Casement's Last Adventure. (1932). p132.

(43) Ellis, John. Diary of a Hangman. 1996. p5.

(44) Monteith, Captain Robert. Casement's Last Adventure. (1932). p143.

(45) Ibid. p132.

(46) Breen, Dan. My Fight for Irish Freedom. p187.

(47) Barrett, Joe. Diary entries.

(48) Kerry's Fighting Story. (1947)

(49) Carbery's Annual (1947)

(50) Booklet of Austin Stack's GAA Club, Tralee. Street of Champions.

BIBLIOGRAPHY

Barrett, Mary. *St, Raphael's Magdalen Asylum, Tralee. A Case Study*. Unpublished Thesis. October, 1996.

Barrington, T.J. *Discovering Kerry*. Published by The Blackwater Press, Dublin. 1976.

Barry, John and Horan Eamon. *Years of Glory*. Published by the Authors. April, 1977.

Barry, Tom. *Guerilla Days in Ireland*. Published by The Irish Press 1949. Republished by The Mercier Press Limited, Cork. 1955 and Anvil Books, 1962-1995.

Bennett, Richard. *The Black and Tans*. Published by E. Hulton & Co. Ltd. London. 1959.

Bowyer Bell, J. *The Secret Army*. Published by Poolbeg Press Limited. Dublin. 1970.

Breen, Dan. *My Fight for Irish Freedom*. First Published by Talbot Press. 1924. Anvil Books, Dublin. 1993.

Broeker, Galen. *Rural Disorder and Police Reform in Ireland 1812-1836*. Published by Routledge and Keegan. London 1970.

Carbery. *Famous Captains*. Published by Carbery Publications, 35 Dartmouth Square, Dublin. 1947.

Coogan, Tim Pat. *The IRA*. First Published by Pall Mall Press Limited, London. 1970. Published by Harper Collins, London. 1993.

Cousens, S. H. *Regional Death Rates in Ireland during the Great Famine, from 1846 to 1851 in Population Studies, xiv, no. 1*, July 1960. pp55-74.

Cullen, L.M. *An Economic History of Ireland since 1660*. London. 1972. p 132.

Curran, Jim. *The Munster GAA Story*. Printed by Clare Champion, Ennis, Co. Clare.

Cusack, Mary Frances. *History of Ireland.* First published 1868. Published by Studio Editions Limited, U.K. 1995.

Daly, Mary E. *The Operations of Famine Relief, 1945-57, in The Great Irish Famine.* ed Porteir. R.T.E./Mercier. Dublin 1995.

De Burca, Marcus. *The GAA, A History.* Published by Cumann Luthchleas Gael, Croke Park, Dublin 3. 1980.

De Burca, Marcus. *Michael Cusack and the GAA.* Published by Anvil Books, Dublin. 1989.

Donnelly, James Jnr. *A New History of Ireland. Vol V. Ireland Under The Union 1801 - 1870.* Ed. W.E. Vaughan. New York, (1989).

Douglas, John. *Observations on the necessity of a legal provision for the Irish Poor.* Wakeham. Dublin, 1828.

Dwyer, Ryle. *McEllistrim Secrets.* In a series of newspaper articles, The Kerryman, August 19, 1994.

Ellis, John. *Diary of a Hangman.* Published by True Crime Library, P.O. Box 158, London SE20 7QA.

Farrell, Michael. *Northern Ireland; The Orange Free State.* Published by Pluto Press, London. 1980.

Fingall, Lady Elizabeth. *Seventy Years Young.* Published by Collins, London 1937.

Finnane, *Mark. Insanity and the Insane in Post-Famine Ireland.* Croom Helm. London. 1981.

Fogarty, Michael. Ryan, Liam. Lee, Joseph. *Irish Values and Attitudes.* Dominican Publications. Dublin 1984.

Gaughan, J. Anthony. *Austin Stack, Portrait of a Separatist.* Published by Kingdom Books, Dublin. 1977.

Gaughan, J. Anthony. *Listowel and Its Environs.* Mercier Press, Cork 1973

Geary, Laurence. *Famine, Fever and the Bloody Flux, in The Great Irish Famine.* ed, Cathal Porteir. RTE/Mercier. Dublin 1995. pp74-85.

Hall, Mr. & Mrs. S.C. *Hall's Ireland.* Condensed Edition published by Sphere Books Limited. 1984.

Harrington, Niall C. *Kerry Landing.* Published by Anvil Books Limited, Dublin. 1982.

Herlihy, Jim. *The Royal Irish Constabulary.* Published by Four Courts Press, Fumbally Lane, Dublin 8.

Hopkinson, Michael. *Green against Green.* Published by Gill and Macmillan, Dublin. 1982.

Kelliher, Margaret. *Irish Famine in Literature, in The Great Irish Famine.* ed. Cathal Porteir. RTE/Mercier Press. Dublin, 1995. pp232-247.

Kelly, Lucid and O'Sullivan. *Blennerville, Gateway to Tralee's Past.* (1989)

Kinealy, Christine. *The Role of the Irish Poor Law during the Famine, in The Great Irish Famine .* ed. Cathal Porteir. Dublin. (1995).

Laxton, Edward. *The Famine Ships.* Published by Bloomsbury Publishing, London. 1996.

Lee, Joe. *The Modernisation of Irish Society 1848-1918.* Gill and Macmillan. Dublin 1973.

Lee, Joseph. *Marriage and Population Growth in Pre-Famine Ireland. Economic and History Review. 2nd Series xxi.* 1968.

Macardle, Dorothy. *Tragedies of Kerry.* Published by Irish Freedom Press, Dublin. 1991.

Mac Aonghusa, Proinsias. *Quotations from P.H Pearse.* Published by Mercier, Cork and Dublin. 1979.

MacEoin, Uinseann. *The Survivors*. Published by Argenta Publications, Dublin. 1980.

Mac Eoin, Uinseann. *The IRA in the Twilight Years*. Published by Argenta Publications. Dublin. 1997.

MacLysaght W. *The Great Famine in Kerry. 18/10/1958*. In a series of articles in The Kerryman, October-November 1958.

McMorran, Russel. *Short history and guide to Tralee and environs*. Published by McMorran. Tralee. 1980.

Manning, Maurice. *The Blueshirts*. Published by Gill and Macmillan Ltd., Dublin. 1971.

Minute of Poor law Commission, quoted in the Report of the Royal Commission on the Poor Laws and Relief of Distress - Report on Ireland, 1909. (4630), xxxvii p 13.

Monteith, Capt. Robert. *Casement's Last Adventure*. Published by The Irish People Monthly, Chicago. 1932.

Murphy, John A. *Ireland in the Twentieth Century*. Published by Gill and Macmillan, Dublin. 1975.

Neeson, Eoin. *The Civil War 1922-23*. Published by Poolbeg Press, Dublin. 1989.

O'Connor, Ulick. *The Troubles. The Struggle for Irish Freedom 1912-1922*. Published by Mandarin Paperbacks, London. 1989.

O'Donovan, Donal. *Kevin Barry and His Time*. Published by The Glendale Press, Dublin. 1989.

O'Dwyer, Michael. *Tralee. A Historical Guide*. Published by O'Dwyer. N.D.

O'Faolain, Sean. *King of The Beggars. A Life of Daniel O'Connell*. Published by Poolbeg Press, Dublin. 1995.

O'Faolain, Sean. *The Irish*. Published by Penguin Books, London. 1980.

O'Malley, Ernie. *On Another Man's Wound*. Published by Anvil Books Limited, Dublin. 1990.

O'Malley, Ernie. *The Singing Flame.* Published by Anvil Books Limited, Dublin. 1992.

O'Mahony, Sean. *Frongoch. University of Revolution.* Published by FDR Teoranta, Dublin. 1987.

O'Neill, Thomas P. (The Earl of Longford). *Eamon De Valera.* Published by Gill and Macmillan, Dublin. 1970.

Pearse, Padraic. *The Murder Machine and Other Essays.* Published by The Mercier Press, Dublin. 1986.

Puirseal, Padraig. *The GAA In Its Time.* Published by Purcell Family, Dublin. 1982.

Reidy, D.A. *St John's Church and the parish of Tralee.* Tralee N.d.

Ryan, Meda. *The Tom Barry Story.* Published by Mercier Press Limited, Dublin. 1982.

Smith, Raymond. *Gaelic Games, The Complete Handbook.* Published by Sporting Books Publishers, Dublin. 1988.

The Freeman's Journal, March 31st, 1923. (Excerpts).

The GAA. Historical Documents, National Library of Ireland.

Woodham-Smith, Cecil. *The Great Hunger.* Published by Oldtown Books, New York. 1989.

Index